MW01273336

Authors' addresses

Postal address

Suite 135
138-1876 Cooper Rd.,
Kelowna, BC
V1Y 9N6

e-mail address:
neverhangwallpaper@yahoo.ca

Editorial services by Ann Hatfield, Galloping Pen Writing and Editing Service, gallopingpen@shuswap.net

Note for Librarians: A cataloguing record for this book is available from Library and Archives Canada at www.collectionscanada.ca/amicus/index-e.html
ISBN 1-4120-9449-6

Printed in Victoria, BC, Canada. Printed on paper with minimum 30% recycled fibre.
Trafford's print shop runs on "green energy" from solar, wind and other environmentally-friendly power sources.

Offices in Canada, USA, Ireland and UK

Book sales for North America and international:
Trafford Publishing, 6E–2333 Government St.,
Victoria, BC V8T 4P4 CANADA
phone 250 383 6864 (toll-free 1 888 232 4444)
fax 250 383 6804; email to orders@trafford.com
Book sales in Europe:
Trafford Publishing (UK) Limited, 9 Park End Street, 2nd Floor
Oxford, UK OX1 1HH UNITED KINGDOM
phone +44 (0)1865 722 113 (local rate 0845 230 9601)
facsimile +44 (0)1865 722 868; info.uk@trafford.com
Order online at:
trafford.com/06-1204

10 9 8 7 6 5 4 3

Never Hang Wallpaper
With
Your wife

From wallpapering to stripping paint–a humorous and informative book of ideas and stories about home repairs and the joys of decorating with your wife

Laugh while you learn.

by
Michael C. Hammar and William S. Peckham

Photographs–Lynn Vaughan Illustrations–George Balabar

To Ken
Hope you enjoy the humour.
W. Peckham

Michael C. Hammar

Never Hang Wallpaper
With
Your wife

Dear Reader:

Never Hang Wallpaper with Your Wife is a book that will have you laughing as you learn. The stories and tips are based on my experiences, over fifty years, in the home repair and renovation field. This book is designed to help you find a solution to your home repair or renovation problem.

I have told most of these stories on home show stages across the country, on local and national television and on radio shows. They have been written for newspapers and magazines and now they are compiled here, in book form, for you to enjoy and use.

Laugh, learn and enjoy.

William G. Beckham

Michael C. Hammar

Important Safety Warning

This book is not intended to take the place of a qualified and trained professional. Each reader is urged to take the necessary precautions when undertaking any do-it-yourself fix-it task. You are strongly urged to read the manufacturers' instructions and safety warnings, carefully, on the packages of materials and the instructions, which accompany tools. The author and the publisher advise you that the manufacturer's instructions and safety warnings supersede anything written in this book. Call in a professional if the task at hand exceeds your capabilities or skills. Although all care has been taken to ensure information in this book is accurate, neither the author nor publisher is responsible for accidents, injuries, or damages incurred as a result of repairs or projects undertaken by you, the reader.

Forward

by

Terry Stephenson

Former Director of Marketing for Stanley Tools of Canada

Although I was marketing director for Stanley Tools of Canada, for several years, and am familiar with the tools for construction, I am the first to admit I am not a good handyman. My skills are lacking when it come to hands-on. I have friends, relatives, and even a contractor buddy, who are very handy. When I asked them for advice they usually told me to hire a handyman or contractor. Before I met Michael Hammar, in 1990, I would have done that very thing.

Michael Hammar is a man who knows all the shortcuts and tricks of the contractor trade. He was actually able to explain them in plain everyday language I could understand.

In my capacity as Director of Marketing for Stanley Tools of Canada I had worked extensively with Michael, hiring him to preview tools, on his national television show and to the public at Home Shows and Wood Shows across Canada. Michael's easygoing approachable manner and sympathetic ear ensured his presentations were always well attended.

It was during this time Michael discussed numerous projects he had in mind for his retirement, not the least of which was to write a do it yourself-er's guide to the shortcuts and tricks of the trade… with stories of his own mistakes and blunders. I was more than pleased, if only for selfish reasons, to hear Michael had *"Never Hang Wallpaper With Your Wife"* as his first project.

Michael's easy, straightforward way of telling things makes this book fun and informative to read. I know you will get some good ideas, tips and lots of chuckles and laughs as well. You might even see yourself in some of the situations Michael describes—I know I did!

Terry Stephenson

Never Hang Wallpaper With your Wife
One Man's Labour of Love

This book is dedicated to:

My late Grandpa Mac, for all he taught me about using my hands to create and using my mind to solve problems.

My late mother and father, for the things they taught me about people, persistence, patience and believing in myself.

Jim, my son, for his help, energy, suggestions, ideas, encouragement and support.

Marilyn Vaughan, my wife, for encouraging me to keep going, her patience, and for reading endless pages of copy, and for helping me make those corrections needed.

Betty, my former wife, for letting me use the stories I have written about the two of us, and the laughs we had while decorating.

The late George Balbar, who created the diagrams through-out the book and helped me maintain an objective outlook.

The late Wayne Farrar, who photographed the handy tips from which George Balbar created the art.

Ann Hatfield, for her many hours of editing and suggestions.

Many people have given me tips over the past thirty years and I wish to thank all of them for their help.

Michael C. Hammar
An Introduction to the Man and his Work

Michael Hammar was born, William (Bill) Peckham, in Niagara Falls, in July of 1931. He was a shy child. No one then could have predicted that he would turn out to be one of Canada's foremost authorities on home renovations and appear on radio, television and stages across Canada.

Bill first worked in the lumber business for nearly 20 years. He worked his way up from yard-hand to marketing and advertising manager of one of Ontario's largest independent retail building centres. Through the coming years he and his wife built their own home and he worked on extensive renovation and decorating projects.

In 1971 Bill, approached a local radio station about hosting a home-renovation radio show. The call-in, home-renovation show was born, the first of its kind in Canada. Bill took the stage name, Michael C. Hammar. His how-to presentations were popular features, every year, in home shows from Vancouver to Halifax.

As Michael Hammar, Bill wrote for magazines and newspapers, broadcast on local radio, wrote and hosted the national television show, Don't Move Improve.

Bill, or Michael, as many will remember him, retired after fifty-two years in the home-improvement field. For nearly thirty of those years he was a broadcaster, writer and entertainer. Bill was a pioneer in his field. And in 2002, like so many other pioneers, Bill moved west–to Kelowna, British Columbia.

He is still performing, but now–as a singer and comedian, with his new wife and partner, Marilyn, at many seniors' homes and retirement villages in the Kelowna area.

Contents

Foreword-By Terry Stephenson, former Director of Marketing for Stanley Tools of Canada.

1 **Chapter One – Never Hang Wallpaper With Your Wife**

The season of discontent a time for decorating and a time to guard the relationship of husband and wife. A journey through the redecorating of a home and some insights into how redecorating can affect a relationship.

2 **Chapter Two – Planning Your Work And Working Your Plan**

Her bathroom… a test of our marriage, or how I did it three times. This story outlines why only one person should be the boss on the job.

3 **Chapter Three – Make Sure You Do It Right!**

My first re-wallpapering experience. Did that paper really shrink three times? The frustrations of wallpapering for the first or even the fifth time. A story about how what you do today can come back to haunt you tomorrow.

4 **Chapter Four – The New House**

Experiences gained from building my first house and something that went bang in the night. Even though I had experience in the lumber business this project showed me just how much I did not know about building. I crammed a lifetime of experiences into just two years.

5 **Chapter Five – My Do It Yourself Misadventures**

Words to make my skin crawl and how I nearly drown in a basement. The myth of saying, "We'll just spend a few bucks on decorating and have a new house." Many handy tips and stories.

Chapter 1

Never Hang Wallpaper with Your Wife.
or
Men and Women See Things Differently!

The Season of Discontent

Spring has passed, and summer is fast approaching… the season that I dread. For me, summertime is the season I dread the most. Oh, the Christmas season is one of hurry, worry, wrap and exchange; Easter is the season to paint and hide eggs, and visit the in-laws; but the summer season, in the home of a school teacher, is the **"The Season of Discontent"**.

My former wife was a schoolteacher at the time these events took place. All of us, who are not schoolteachers, fear the summer season. It is the season we must face with the most apprehension. If I sound just a tiny bit anxious it is because I am. This was the time my wife, bless her heart, contracted that nonfatal disease, which all males fear… "Homeimprovementitis". I know she has finally come down with the annual case of "Homeimprovementitis" when, at the breakfast table one morning in June, she would say, "This summer I would like to freshen up the master bedroom."

Translation: I, her husband, am going to live in hell for at least three weeks while we visit paint stores, pick out colours, hold those little chips of "summer rose" (pink) against swatches of "baby's breath teal" (off green) and ooh and aah about throw cushions, until I could… throw cushions. Watching a gray-haired old man stand in a decorating store and cry is not a pretty sight, believe me. If I could have gotten away with it I would have flopped down on the floor, and thrown a tantrum. That only works for kids under six, but then maybe I was in my second childhood and it might have worked.

As many people know, I was a home improvement "expert". I advised more people in a year on their home improvement problems, at home shows, on television, radio and in print, than you can ever imagine. But, at home was I an "expert"? Nooooooo. My wife sees me, as she put it so succinctly, as being only me. Meaning, I guess, she expects me to think like all other men. In the words of one wiser to the ways of man, "if it ain't broke don't fix it and if it is broke wiggle your way out of fixing it." That is my philosophy exactly.

In the summer of 1989, I sold my shares in my business to my partner, and retired to follow my dream of traveling and sharing my knowledge with people across Canada. My wife decided, since I did not have a real job to keep me busy, we would redecorate our house. I was happy when she confirmed the fact that it was really she and I who were going to redecorate. I figured after 34 years of marriage we should be able to work together. I had forgotten something, which a friend pointed out to me after he read a draft of this book.

"Men and women do not think alike."

That phrase would come back to haunt me over and over again before this decorating stint was done.

"Will this take us long? Can we count on the whole summer or could we figure maybe a couple of weeks?" I queried.

"No, all I want is to put some paint in a couple of rooms and some wallpaper in a couple of the other rooms," she answered.

This seemed fine to me. After all, how long could it take to slap a little paint here and a little paint there? How long could it take? I'll tell you how long… fourteen days, fourteen hours a day–that is how long it took!

"It's six o'clock, honey. Let's get up and at it. We're going to the paint store and the fabric shops today, remember?"

Boy, is she bright-eyed and bushy-tailed this morning.

"Okay! Okay! I'm getting up. I suppose you wished the stores would open at 7:30, so we could get right at it, eh?"

"Well that would be a help, but you don't have to be sarcastic; that's a heck of a way to start our adventure."

With the opening of the stores we set out on our adventure... skipping merrily down the path... to hell.

At this point I would like to make this observation, women and men do not see colours in the same way, and this is grounded in fact. Tests have been done to prove it. I do not mean just that we see colours differently but we view them in an entirely different way. What the paint manufacturer calls dusty rose women call dusty rose, old fashioned rose or rose like that in the carpet. Men call it dirty pink. Now, that is not to say either of us is right or wrong, but just that we view colours differently. When we men say it is dirty rose we are not being derogatory. We simply mean it does not look like the pure innocent pink we remember dressing our daughters in as children. That, of course, was before all the fuss over sex **differentiation**, but that is another whole book.

Since women and men view decorating differently, the search for the ideal paint, paper, broadloom and accessories becomes a war between the sexes. We men do not mean to make it a war. All we want to do is get on with the job of painting, papering and such. Just get it over with, so we can get back to a normal life of puttering in the workshop, playing golf or sitting back and reading a book.

"Hon, I'm not really into paint chips and fabric swatches." I try to weasel my way out of going. "Can't you do that and just let me do the actual work."

"Like picking out the colours and fabrics and such is not work? You think this is easy?"

"No, I don't think it's easy but I do think it would be easier if you didn't have me along, you know, to clutter up the decision making. You're the one who is going to have to be happy with it for the next 15 years or so."

I think you guys will agree. **We** can live with it if **they** can. If we have to go with them, we will, at all cost, avoid positive comments about the colours for fear of offending them. If truth be known, we really do not want to be blamed for the choices years down the road when they are tired of it, or it does not go with something they want to change.

Many of us guys, as the search starts for accessories, have said, "You know, if we had used the paint I wanted to use we would not have had this problem of finding the right coloured cushions. It would go with all the accessories we already have".

But of course, that is why they have changed the paint. They **want** new accessories.

I think many men will agree with me when I say, we have all too often heard this phrase: "You know I really am getting tired of the colour **you** picked for the living room." We have lived with the colour we probably did not like but said okay to, because we thought she liked it.

Here is a tip for the female readers; it comes from many men with whom I have discussed the content of this book.

"Just pick the paint, wallpaper and broadloom and leave us out of it. We'll do the labour work and be done with it. We don't want to be involved with itty-bitty pieces of fabric, paint chips and carpet samples."

There is one thing we men would ask of you, while you are tearing things up and changing colours and furniture. Please, leave "**our**" room alone. "**Our's**" is the one room in the house where we can kick back, put up our feet and be the slobs we long to be all day or all week, while we have to be "presentable" at the office. This could be the TV room, a den, a home office or just a little room we have created at the back of the garage. We do not care if the brown paneling is not the "in" colour or if the gold or avocado shag rug has not been popular for the last 20 years. We like the "feel" of the room and we are comfortable please leave it alone. We beg of you.

The search for paint, paper and broadloom is just a skirmish in the decorating war. The big battle really comes when we start looking for accessories. I think everyone who has ever decorated a house will agree; none of us has a–colour photographic mind. What do I mean by that? Well, here is an example. We decorated our master bedroom with two different papers and we painted the trim off-white, to go with the background of one of the papers. One paper was basically colonial blue and the other was an off white, a beige kind of colour. Each paper had the same small flowers on it. In other words, they were complimentary papers and, yes, we both liked them and still do, even after several years. Amazing is it not? One weekend we went shopping for accessories, cushions, knickknacks and drapery material. On our quest for the right "throw" cushions, we stopped at one of our favorite stores, right in front of a pile of the right sized cushions.

"Let's look through this bin; I know we'll find just what we want and the hunt will be over."

"I'll drink to that," I said.

We rooted through the pile and came up with the exact shade of colonial blue we had in the wallpaper.

"I told you we'd find just what we wanted," she exclaimed.

"Are you sure they're the right blue?"

"Of course, I know what colour blue we have in the paper. After all, I picked the paper out, didn't I?"

We stopped looking for cushions and loaded up the van with our purchases. We could hardly wait to "throw" the cushions on the bed. Now most men, married as long as I have been, know throw means place the cushions, very carefully, on the bed so they look as though they have been thrown there. I have never been able to understand why you just cannot throw the cushions on the bed. If that is the look you want then that, is the way to do it. But I digress.

"Let's get up to the bedroom now," she said breathlessly.

"Okay, I'm right behind you."

"Bring the cushions with you."

Boy was I on the wrong track. We put the cushions in the room next to the colonial wallpaper

"They don't match!"

"I know… what happened?" I asked.

"I don't know. The cushions are a muddy-purpley-blue and the paper colonial blue".

"How could we have been so wrong in our choice?" I asked

We soon realized, after other similar experiences, our memories were not–colour photographic. We did solve this problem and it was easy. A decorator at a home show in Ottawa helped us solve the problem of colour matching. She made it seem so simple.

"Next time you go shopping, take samples of the paint, wallpaper and carpet with you. You'll have no trouble with matching then."

"Now why didn't we think of that?" I said.

I must admit it seemed like a good idea at the time, and so simple.

"I can't find the sample of the wallpaper in my purse. We'll have to go home and get a piece," my wife said.

"All the way home? Let's wait until the next time we go looking for stuff."

"This carrying samples around is really not very convenient. We have to come up with a better plan."

I agreed and started thinking about it.

"I have an idea," she said. "Let's glue the samples to a piece of cardboard."

"Wow! What an idea. I wonder how big a piece of cardboard we should use? How about a small enough piece to fit into the glove compartment? We don't keep gloves in there anyway. Then we'll always have samples with us. I'll make one for your car and one for my van."

I made up two sample boards from foam core; this is available in most art shops and hardware stores. We made two sizes. One was 2-inches by 4-inches, small enough for my wife to carry in her purse. The other was 4-inches by 6-inches in size and carried in our cars. We divided the boards into three parts. On one third of the board we glued a piece of the carpet. On the middle third, we glued the piece of wallpaper and, just above the paper we applied some of the paint used in the room. If we had a second paper used in the room or a border, we glued it on the back of the sample board. We did this for each room we had decorated. Now we were ready to go shopping for accessories for each room.

The reason we made up the smaller sample board was very simple… "expediency". If we were in a store and came across something we thought we might use, in one of our rooms, one of us had to go to the car for the sample board. With a sample board in my wife's purse it can be produced quickly and we knew if the article would be a match.

I like being organized; with these sample boards it meant we were organized and ready to shop for accessories for any of the re-decorated rooms.

"This decorating stuff is not too bad after all… I guess."

Whoa… who said that? Not me I hope. Guys, don't get mad at me.

"Now that we have picked the paint, the paper and the carpet, can we get started dear?" I asked her.

"You sound rather anxious. Are you looking forward, to the new fresh look we'll have when we're finished?"

Well, I was not as anxious to get started, as I was to get finished, if the truth were known.

"Yes, it'll be good to see the fruits of our labours but I would rather see the putting green at Lost Valley Golf Club."

The work part of the redecorating job got started.

"This is going to be a breeze," I mumble under my breath. Can't wait to see how it turns out. I have to admit she has picked some pretty nice paper and paint. I'm not too sure about the carpet, but we'll see.

Get out the drop cloths, ladders, paint trays, brushes, paddles, sponges, sharp knife, bucket, detergent and a washing cloth, it is time to start work.

"Wait a cotton-pick'n minute. Are we going to wash the walls first?"

"Yes", she says. "The walls must be washed clean first".

"I was under the impression we were painting and papering the walls to cover up the slightly dingy surface."

"You can't paint over dirt. You know that. Seems to me I've heard you tell people, on your radio show, to always, always wash first, not to be lazy, and do the job right. I think I've even heard you say. If you don't have time to do it right the first time when will you have time to do it over? Am I right dear?" she says with an all-knowing smile.

Damn; I hate it when she is right. I had not known she listened to my radio show.

Like most guys, I was hoping to get away with just painting and papering. Foiled again by my own quotes. By the way, when you wash the walls with detergent you must rinse with clean water. If you do not, you may leave a film of detergent behind and then the paint will not adhere.

I always use a primer when I paint. By using primer you will find the finish paint will adhere and cover better. I suggest you have the primer tinted a few shades lighter than the final coat. White primer can show through the final coat, especially if you try to spread the paint too thin. By having the primer tinted a couple of shades lighter than the finish coat you will be able to see any spots you might have missed with the finish coat.

Primers do not always cover the same area as the finish coat so check the can for coverage, and buy the correct amount. This could save you an extra trip to the store.

When we bought the paint for the bathroom I asked the sales clerk to mark the colour number on the tin. You will find, as I did, they usually mark it on the top of the tin. This might seem all right at the time but as I found out several years earlier it should be marked on the bottom of the tin.

When we put an addition on the house, several years before, my son Jim, and I did the painting and papering of the walls and ceilings. There were three rooms to the addition, and to speed things up one of us primed one room while the other put the finish coat on another room. We tried to keep all of our paint in one room on a drop cloth; the carpets were not installed yet, so if there were any spills they would be in one room, only. Jim removed the lid from his paint tin and I took the lid off mine and laid it beside Jim's lid on the drop cloth. When we were finished, painting, we picked up the lids and we replaced them on the tins. No problem there, right? Well read on.

"Dad, we need another tin of primer. Could you pick it up on your way home from work tomorrow so I can finish the bathroom priming?"

I looked at the lid on the primer tin and ordered that colour. When I returned home and started to prime the wall the colour seemed darker; it was the exact colour and shade of the finished coat.

"Well I'll be," I said scratching my head.

I had gotten the finish colour not the primer colour. What happened, I wondered? You have probably guessed it already. When we sealed our paint tins the night before I had put the wrong lid on the primer tin. Lesson learned. I have the paint number put on the bottom of the can now. A friend, William, asked me why not have special tags of polymer made so that you can put the colour number on the tag and attach it to the handle. Good idea but it could come off and besides it is easier to turn the can upside down and look at it. Be sure the lid is put on tightly.

The painting went well but then how far wrong can you go with a little paint?

Now wallpaper–that is another story. I think wallpaper is just another name for making a mess in the name of change and it can lead to a strain, to say the least, in any relationship.

First, let me ask you what is wrong with leaving perfectly acceptable wallpaper on the bedroom for several years? I do not think there is anything wrong with that. I mean really!!! You can wash it where it is a little grubby, and put a chest in front of the spot with the tear in it. Right? Wrong!

There is someone in my family who thinks paper should be changed every three or four years. Put together a woman who wants the paper changed every couple of years and a bullheaded, stubborn know-it-all man who thinks it is okay the way it is and you have trouble brewing. The stress in the atmosphere is so thick you can almost touch it.

On this particular Saturday, I condescended to put the paper up. We were working along fairly well; (that means I had not had to take too many pieces of paper down to match up that invisible speck in the pattern) when things began to get difficult.

Translation: I was getting tired, slopping water on the floor and I was not listening. Something was bound to snap.

I was at the top of the stepladder, she was urging me to come down, step back and look at the bad match of the pattern. I came down the ladder all right and she said, "watch!"

"I know how to come down a ladder," I snapped.

Then it happened, I stepped right on the edge of the wallpaper water-tray. It flipped up, soaked me and I fell on the floor into the puddle getting even wetter. That did it, game over. She laughed her head off while I fumed. The papering ended for that day and I sat down, and… well you can guess the rest. You know, it really was funny when you look back on it but I have never admitted it to her to this day.

Whenever she starts to tell that story to friends I just say "Dear should I tell them about the time you sewed the pocket of a pair of slacks to the leg?"

The next day we decided to finish the wallpapering. That is when everything came unhinged. Things were going well enough until we hit the middle of the first wall and that is when she said, "The pattern doesn't match. Lift it up on the right side a little."

"I don't see anything wrong with the match."

"Just look for yourself–and put on your glasses–it's as plain as the nose on your face. The little pink dot next to the green leaf is not lined up with the dot on the second sheet."

Let me say here, I try to live by the rule that I must satisfy the boss at all cost. But when the mismatch happened on every piece we put up I decided to change and live by son Jim's rule–"good enough at ten." That means if you cannot see the mistake at ten feet it is "good enough".

"Dear, you know I like to do things the way you want them done. I make every effort to please you in these tiny things but I think it's time to invoke Jim's rule "good enough at ten."

"What the heck is that rule all about?" she said.

When I explained Jim's rule she asked me for a demonstration. Sooooo, I took out my measuring tape slid it out across the floor to the 10 foot mark.

"Stand here ten feet away from the wall and look at the paper. Can you see the miss-match on the wallpaper? Can you see the non-alignment of pink dots?"

"No," she retorted angrily.

"Well, 'Good enough'," I said.

As you can probably guess, this did not go over very well and I paid for it the rest of the day.

We had worked all day on that room and were just putting up the last piece of border; it was a long piece. I was on a ladder; she was on a stool. I was smoothing the border along the wall and she was holding the loose end up for me. The phone rang.

"Leave it for the machine," I said. This was in the days before voice mail.

She said, "I'll get it and be right back".

There I stood, holding that wet, cold, sticky piece of border. When she let go of her end, of the border, it began to slowly come away from the wall. All I could do was stand there, and watch it, and hope she would come back before it was wrapped around my head. She did not. When she finally got back all she could do was stand and laugh. I was stuck there with the dripping, gooey, messy border wrapped around my neck and down my back. I was not a happy camper.

"Who was on the phone that was so damned important?"

"It was Anna from Sudbury and I just couldn't say I'd call her back," she commented with a sweet smile. "So sorry about that."

Over the years my wife had some good laughs at my expense; in retrospect these happenings were funny, really.

By the way, I got even with Anna a few months later when I was at a home show in Sudbury, doing my thing. With Anna and her friends sitting in the front row of the audience, I told the story of the paper border and the phone call; then I had Anna stand up. "Gotcha Anna."

This is why I say, "Never Hang Wallpaper with your wife".

Chapter 2

Planning Your Work and Working Your Plan

We were nearly finished this little foray into redecorating, and the end was in sight. I was eager to finish. Although there had been words, nasty looks, as well as huffs and puffs, sometimes, we had not actually had a "fight". Well, not yet, anyway.

This next room would really test the marriage. We were about to *do* her bathroom.

The words I had heard from my wife were, "We'll need only a little paint in here, and maybe we could put some wallpaper on the end wall: nothing too fancy".

I had heard those words before, so I was ready for a complete makeover.

We painted the wall–that was okay–no arguments there. Sure we had a few discussions, about what colour beige was, pinky beige or brownie beige. Next, we decided to put that very simple wallpaper on the end wall.

"There'll be no matching to do with this paper," my wife said.

"Ha!" was all I could say.

The papering went reasonably well. Only had to pull the second piece off twice to get it matched up to an invisible pink spot in the pattern, which only my wife could see. There was to be no match-ing, she said, but that little pink spot came back to haunt me with every piece I applied. When the papering was done we stepped back and admired our work.

I breathed a sigh of relief when she said, "There, doesn't that look great, and, I think we are done… but wait, (I would hear this phrase many times during this project) wouldn't the vanity look better with a new set of faucets?"

I agreed and suggested we change the sink and countertop along with the backsplash while we were at it. Then we would not have to do the job twice.

"No, no, that won't be necessary, just the faucets."

Off we went on a hunt for that perfect set of faucets.

I had demonstrated faucets for a faucet manufacturer, at home shows and trade shows and I should know my faucets. Right? Wrong! What did I know about those very special faucets, the ones that would set off the bathroom like a new piece of jewelry on a ball gown? We prowled the discount stores, the classy top-line stores, then, dragged ourselves back to the discount stores. Finally, we settled for a set of single-lever pullout faucets, in chrome.

Home we went; I was finally seeing the light at the end of the tunnel. I took out the old faucets. The workers who had installed the old faucets, in my mind, were not skilled plumbers because they soldered the faucets into the water lines, instead of using the usual hand-tightened nuts with shut off valves. There was no easy way to install the new faucets but I did it, in about two hours, rearranging some plumbing at the same time. Then I called my wife to come and take a look.

"Now isn't that better? It's just perfect. But..." (here it comes again) "I think we need a new vanity sink."

"How about a new countertop with a backsplash? That way we'll be finished for sure," I said.

"No, no just a sink," came back to me.

Well, the trek was on... again. Finally, she spotted a china sink, not your ordinary vanity sink, a china sink. It weighed about 50 pounds, I am sure. By the way, if you can afford a china sink, for my money, they cannot be beaten. They are heavy but solid and well-made and they will not rust or chip.

I had to take out that new set of faucets, cut a bigger hole in the counter, silicone in the new sink; and install the faucets, for the second time. I had to rearrange the plumbing again, because the sink was larger.

We stepped back and admired our work, and once again, I heard, "Now isn't that better? It's just perfect, but… the vanity counter-top **is** rather scruffy looking; let's get a new one."

No! I did not say, "I suggested that, before we got started, but you said, 'Oh, no, that was not necessary'".

Off we went again, on a mission. The light at the end of the tunnel had faded quickly.

The old vanity was a built-in-place one and was slightly deeper than the standard type, so, we had to buy a kitchen counter top and cut it down to size. Since we had ceramic tile as a back splash I had to cut the formed-backsplash off to fit below it, you know that part at the back of the countertop that goes up the wall. I tore out the new faucets for the second time; then pulled out the vanity sink. I ripped out the old counter top, which had been built in place with aluminum trim at the back, with about four hundred nails holding it down. The installers must have thought it would blow away in a heavy wind or they had shares in a nail-manufacturing plant.

When I had installed the new counter, I cut the opening for the china sink… applied more caulking and set it in place–for the second time. Then, I installed the new faucets for the third time, and re-did the plumbing. More copper pipe had to be added and more drainpipe, as well. Now we were finished. On second thought, maybe not.

When the boss came to inspect I heard those words again.

"Now isn't that better? Just perfect… but..."

"No buts!" I was adamant here.

I explained, that if I had to remove the ceramic tile I would have to change the plumbing again. And, if I took the ceramic tile off the wall at the back, we would have to buy another counter top, one with a back splash on it just like the one I had just sawn off–not very cost effective!

Finally, the job was over. It actually took me four weeks and several hundred dollars to do that 'decorating' job which had been estimated, by the foreperson, to take only a few days and a 'couple' of bucks, at the most. All in all, I installed those faucets three times and that sink twice.

I must admit, it did look quite good; but do not tell my wife I said that.

I never know when we start a project, just how long it will take or how much it will cost. The reason is, one of us cannot plan well enough in advance to make those estimates work.

I took course one time on planning my time. During that course, the instructor gave us some very good advice, which I have tried to keep in mind as I wandered through life. "Plan your work and work your plan." We could have saved hours of time on this job if we had looked at the overall project and planned our work. "We" would have saved time, on travel as well as installation, but who am I to question anyone. I am just the home improvement "expert" in the family.

Chapter 3

Make Sure You Do it Right!

Early in our marriage I watched my wife and her mother wall-paper our living room. That was in the days of mixing paste and spreading it on the back of the paper with big brushes–smoothing the paper on the wall and catching the excess paste before it hit the floor. Not a job I would want to tackle. But, then came prepasted wallpaper and I was anxious to try papering.

Let me tell you about my first wallpaper job. My wife wanted the wall in the television room covered with wallpaper. Hanging pre-pasted paper looked easy and I was itching to get started on a job, honestly I was, but… I did not want to do it with the family around. There would be too many bosses and too many embarrassing moments, if I goofed up.

The bottom half of the wall was panelling, with a shelf to divide the panelling from the wallpaper above. It should be a simple job, done in one evening. Cut the pre-pasted wallpaper, wet it and put it in place. Right? Wrong! I had primed the drywall earlier with white primer, now that was a mistake, but that is a story for later. I put the paper in place, smoothed it out, taking care not to stretch it, and left it to dry. Our son Jim was the first to arrive home. I was sitting in the living room watching TV.

"Jim, come on down to the TV room and see what I did to-night".

Proud as a new papa showing off his baby, I showed him the wallpaper job.

"Are those white stripes supposed to be there at each joint?"

"Off to bed young man, and don't say a word to your mom in the morning. I'll look after this."

The paper was still damp so I took it down and put it back in place with the edges just touching, being very careful not to stretch it.

"Hi, there." Our daughter had just come into the house. "Come see what I did this evening."

Confidently, I walked her downstairs and showed her my work.

"It looks great, Dad," she said laughing. "Especially the white stripes at the joints. Quite an idea, really quite up-beat."

The paper had shrunk again, or so I thought. Still damp, so down it came. I repapered again and when my wife came home I thought, this cannot happen a third time.

"Did you get the papering done in the TV room tonight?" my wife asked.

"Yep. Wanna see it?" was my reply.

"What are those white stripes for? They weren't in the paper were they?" again the question.

"No!" I responded.

I was furious with the paper manufacturer. I found out later, when I returned the paper to the store, it was entirely the fault of the paper, a production defect, and not mine. However, you can have this happen with perfectly good paper if you smooth too much or press too hard. Both will stretch the paper; then it does shrink as it dries.

If I had primed with a dark paint, to match the paper, any shrinkage would have been hidden. The primer showing through the cracks would have matched the colour of the paper. If you do prime in white there is something else you can do to cover the white where the joint will be. Mark the wall where the edge of each piece of paper will be. Use a wide, dark-coloured felt tip marker and put a stripe down the wall at this point.

By the way, this trick works with wood panelling as well. Put the dark stripe on the stud and, if the panelling shrinks a little, the pale stud will not show between the panels.

When I put up plywood, veneered-hardboard or composite-board panelling I like to store it in the room in which it will be installed, with strips of wood between each sheet, for a few days to allow it to become "acclimatized". I have found that if the panelling is moister than the room when installed, it can shrink as it dries to the room conditions. Conversely, if the panelling is drier than the room, it can swell and buckle as it takes on the humidity of the room. I think you can imagine what the wall would look like either way.

A few years after we moved into our house we built a family room and bathroom in the lower level of our house. The family room was small and cozy and the bathroom too was small. I mean really small. How small was it? It was so small I could sit on the toilet and wash my hands in the sink across from me. It did, however, have a toilet, vanity, shower stall and a small shelf-unit above the toilet. I think we probably could have carpeted it with three large carpet samples like the ones you see in the sample book in the stores.

"The drywall needs to be primed first. I better go and get some primer," I said to my wife.

"Why don't you use the cans of leftover wall paint we have in the basement," she suggested.

"Good idea. No need to buy new paint. It doesn't matter if I use a couple of colours, we're going to paper over it any way."

I was smart–I thought. After all I was an expert in this field. It was all latex paint, cleans up easily and dries in no time.

"I have the priming finished so I'll paper before I put the toilet, vanity and the shelf-unit in place. It'll save a lot of cutting," I called up stairs.

"Go for it. How long will you be? I want to start supper."

"I'll wait until after supper. It might take longer than I anticipate," I said.

Papering before I installed anything was smart thinking right? Yes, very smart.

And, so the bathroom was finished and we used it for several years without the need for a change.

Eventually the time for a change did come. My business partner was getting married. I was his best man and I decided to have some of the boys over to celebrate, just a few drinks and steaks in the backyard: nothing fancy.

"I think if you are having the boys over for a party the downstairs bathroom needs to be spruced up," my wife commented.

"Okay. I'll wash the walls, the shower and shampoo the carpet," was my reply.

"I had a little more than that in mind," was her comment.

I wonder what this is going to entail? Probably some paint on the wall around the shower and maybe a new carpet.

"What did you have in mind?" What a fool I was to ask that question.

"Just some new decorating... wallpaper, carpet, and paint the vanity and shelf-unit over the toilet," was her direction.

"Why don't you do it while I am taking that computer course in a couple of weeks. It shouldn't be a big deal."

"Okay. But does it need all that work?" another silly question. When will I ever learn? Just do it and get it over with.

But I kept putting it off, you know, like we guys do. What else is new, eh? I was hoping I would not have to do the papering and carpeting.

"Please have the bathroom done when I get back, darling."

"Right you are, don't sweat it. Have a good time and I'll see you in a week."

So, my wife went away to take that course for a week, leaving me in charge of the decorating. Just strip the paper off and put on new. Slap a carpet down and away we go. I had papered the walls before the toilet, vanity and shelf-unit were installed? I now had to take all of those fixtures out to take the paper off. And remember the latex paint I used for priming years earlier on the walls? How clever I thought I was using up the ends of old paint.

"@#$%#$%&, gosh darn the paper won't come off the wall cleanly."

The water-based wallpaper glue had gone through the latex paint and was adhering to the paper on the drywall. Naturally some of the drywall paper came off with the wallpaper, tearing out some chunks of drywall

Ring... ring. "Hello."

"Hi! It's me. How's the bathroom coming?"

"Oh! Just fine–no problems."

"Will it be done when I get home?"

"Well probably but..."

"No probablys. Just get it done... please."

"Okay." At least she said please.

The walls looked as though they had been through the gunfight at the OK Coral. This meant I had to remove the drywall. See what I mean when I say sometimes renovations create a domino effect. One thing leads to another. Keep in mind my wife was away for a week and I had left this job until it was nearly time for her to come home. So, what else is new? I was sure I would not be finished in time, and I was not.

To remove the drywall I had to remove the suspended ceiling, the toilet, vanity and shelf-unit and start from scratch. It was prime the drywall–the right way this time, put the suspended ceiling back up, paper, put on a border, carpet, reinstall the toilet, vanity, and shelf-unit. In short: rebuild the bathroom.

My wife arrived home, just as I was installing the carpet in the bathroom.

"Are you just putting the carpet down now?"

"Yes, but I did have a little trouble getting it cut to shape. It took longer than I thought it would take."

Do not lie just tell the bare facts and she will never guess what happened.

"You did a very nice job dear. Thanks for getting it done I'll feel so much better when the boys come for the party. I see some marks on the suspended ceiling channel. What caused that?"

Careful how you answer this, it could come back to bite you.

"Let me get the carpet down, the boys will be here in about an hour and I need to shower and change." Got around that nicely.

Notice I did not say I would tell her later. Take note guys, this is a handy tip but you cannot put it in your written notes on "How To or How Not To".

Painting or Papering Over Wallpaper

There comes a time when you do not want that old wallpaper around any more, so you decide to paint over it. I hope you will think again. If you are planning to paint a wall or a room, which has wallpaper on it, you must begin by removing the old wallpaper and filling the cracks in the plaster. (There are some exceptions and we will talk about those later.)

Painting over old wallpaper can lead to grief. Any air under the old paper will likely create bubbles that will not disappear, after you have painted. Once the bubbles have risen, the paint dries and hardens. This will leave you with a sculptured wall or at the very least one, which might look like lunar landscape. If you paint over old wallpaper and you do have the bubble problem there is no repair. You will have to remove the old paper. With the paint on the paper it will be ten times harder to get off, than it would have been if you had removed it first.

Whether you plan to paper the walls or paint them, you should remove the old paper. I know there will be people who will tell you, "I paper over paper all the time and have had no problems". Well, go look at their paper job, and see if it is as smooth as they say.

There are glues or wallpaper pastes you might try, but most manufacturers will tell you to remove the old paper. If you paper over paper, the bond will not be good and the seams may start to peel and open up. There is another reason for removing the old paper: when you do decide to paint the room one day, and you have to remove two or three layers of paper, you will remember this advice and wish you had heeded it.

Removing old paper can be messy, but if you go about it the right way, it can be a straightforward job. If it is old paper of the type that will absorb water easily, and it was glued on the wall over an oil-based primer, you can wet it, or steam it, and peel it right off. Steamers are usually available at a tool rental outlet or may be available at the wallpaper dealer's store. I know I have made this seem easy, and it can be, if you take your time and use the proper tools.

If it is vinyl paper on the wall, it has its own glue and this glue does not dissolve easily. You may have to score the paper to get the steam under it to reach the glue. After the paper is off you might find there is an under-paper on the wall. This paper is put on to cover old cracked plaster. Sometimes the remaining paper is the backing from dry-strippable paper. I have been told this paper should come off before you paper again, and it must come off if you are going to paint.

"Dear, the paper you put on in here a few years back is looking a little tired these days. Let's paper over it," I heard from the TV room.

"We need to take the old paper off the wall, before we put up new," I reminded her.

"Remember what happened in the bathroom when you did that before your partner's stag? Will the same thing happen here?" (She eventually dragged the story, of the bathroom rebuild, out of me, guys, sorry to say.)

"Good point. We don't want to be forced to re-drywall that room, do we?" I said.

"Why not paper over the old stuff? Can it do any harm?" she asked.

I was caught in a dilemma. It would be easier to paper over the old paper, because it would be quicker than removing it, but doing this went against everything I had learned about wallpapering. I know I should take it off, but….

"Why don't we talk to George at the paint store? He may know of something we can do to avoid removing the old paper."

Good move. If George says we can paper over the old paper and we do and it fails, she can blame George, not me.

He recommended a new primer, which had just come onto the market recently. He said it would work, and you know what–it did. It was a lot of work priming and then putting on new paper but it looked good when we were done.

I have not been in that house in several years now, but when I last saw it the paper was on solid and looked very good. There are, how-ever, two drawbacks: the priming took a long time and cost extra and, when you do decide to take the paper off, and you will eventu-ally, the primer will keep you from steaming the old paper off the wall. The paint and underlying paper will have to be scored and the steam forced under. Not an easy job.

So, Your Trim Looks like it has the Measles, eh?

When you are finished painting the walls and ceiling and ready to sit down to have a cold one, does someone say, "Dear the trim is all speckled looking and it feels rough. What caused that? It looks like flecks of paint."

"It is flecks of paint and I was going to clean them off tomorrow when I was not so tired. Is that okay with you?"

"Well, it does look messy and unfinished. Could you do it to-night?"

"Guess so," I say grouchily. I wanted to see the golf game on TV but the paint specks must come first.

"And there's some on the hardwood floor near the wall too."

When using a roller flecks of paint can splatter the trim and the floor. They are small splatters but they do show up. Jim, our son, was a house painter when he was putting himself through school and he learned a trick, which has served us both well over the years.

If you catch the specks while they are still wet you can use a damp cloth to wipe them off the trim. For latex paint dampen the cloth with water, for oil-base paint dampen the cloth with paint thinner.

But, you may not notice most of the specks until after the painting has been completed and dried. Now you have a different problem. A cloth dampened with water or paint thinner will not budge the dried paint. You are in trouble now. Can you live with that look or with someone reminding you of the mess every now and then?

Do you have to live with it? No!

Jim taught me this very simple method to remove paint specks. He found, with **extra fine** steel wool, rubbing alcohol and a little elbow grease the specks would come off easily. It seems alcohol softens the paint, on the varnish or polyurethane clear coating, to the point that the steel wool removes it. This works with both oil and latex paint splatters. If the varnish or polyurethane clear coating is really quite old, or if you rub too hard, it may dull the shine. It is a good idea to put a thin coat of polyurethane over the old clear finish, after it has been cleaned. Test first to see if the old varnish is compatible with the polyurethane. This is done by brushing on a small patch of the poly in an inconspicuous place. Let it stand for the recommended drying time and then run your finger over it. If it is sticky or gummy it is not compatible, and you will have to find something else to put on the surface. If it is smooth and dry then go ahead and apply a thin coat of poly to the rest of the trim. It will look like new and you will be a hero. To speed up your job and to make cleanup quicker, try water-based or rub-on poly.

Speed Cleaning Paint Brushes and Rollers

"It's time to redecorate again, dear. It's been three months since we did this room," my wife informs me. (I'm exaggerating a little of course.)

Wallpapering I do not mind, but painting, to say the least, is a pain in the… neck.

"What are we going to do now?" I asked

"Paint the master bedroom. It hasn't been painted since we put the addition on several years ago. I want to change the look. We can leave the paper but redo the paint."

"You know I hate painting."

The biggest draw back to painting, in my mind, is the clean up part… especially cleaning the brushes.

About twenty years ago I was in a paint store with my wife, while she was selecting something-or-other I was poking around the store. Just poking around is one of my favorite pastimes; you never know what you will find of interest in a store. I came across an interesting tool. As it turned out it was the answer to my brush-cleaning problem.

"Wow! Look at this thing, dear. My dirty paint brush problems are over."

"What is it?" she asked with a quizzical look on her face.

"A paint-brush spinner," was my reply.

Getting all of the paint out of the brush, and getting it dry after, can be a big headache. The paintbrush spinner can be one of the most useful tools in your tool chest. It has a set of spring jaws on one end and a pump handle, like the handle on a kids spinning top, on the other end. To dry the brush put the brush handle into the spring jaws and, while holding it in an empty 20-liter container, pump the handle up and down. Because of the twisted shaft on the handle the brush spins like a top throwing all of the liquid out of the bristles by centrifugal force. Believe me, it works extremely well. I still do not like painting, but I can, when I have to paint, get the brushes clean. This means I can use good brushes and do a better job.

After getting the brush clean and dry, wrap it in newspaper or a paper towel, folding and creasing the paper to the shape of the brush. Fold the excess paper, at the bristle end of the brush, toward the handle. Be sure not to fold the end of the bristles while doing this. Hang the brush in the workshop to dry. I usually hang brushes on nails up between the joists; the air is warmer there and drying takes place faster. The paper absorbs any dampness and wicks it out to the surface for evaporation. The brush is now ready for the next time.

You can clean and dry a paint roller the same way. Slip the roller over the springs on the top of the spinner and spin the roller dry. However, when storing the roller do not wrap it in paper. Put a three to four inch nail into the side of the floor joists, overhead, in the workshop, slide the roller over the nail and store it there until next time. Remember to shake the dust off the roller before using it again. If you lay the roller on a shelf, instead of hanging it up, it will dry with a flat spot where it sat on the shelf. The next time you use the roller it will leave lines, on your painted surface from the flat spot.

I was watching television one day because a friend of mine, a paint adviser for a very large paint manufacturer, was on a popular decorating show. The host was asking all the right questions and getting the right answers until she asked my friend, "How do you get a paint brush really clean without making a mess?"

"Use a paint brush spinner, (she showed the spinner) spin the brush dry and then store it."

"How should I store the brush?" the host queried.

I shuddered when I heard the answer.

"The brush is only damp now… just put it back into the little plastic sleeve in which you received it from the store", she stated.

I really wanted to jump into the TV and ask her what she had been smoking.

I hollered at the TV, "If you put a damp brush back into the plastic sleeve the brush will mildew. You'll never have to look for it again because you'll only have to follow your nose to find it."

Never, never put the brush back into that plastic sleeve until it is completely dry.

Skin on Top of Oil-based Paint can be an Ugly Mess

"What the heck is this?" I asked myself. When I opened the partially used can of oil-based paint there was a thick skin on the top.

Now that's going to be messy to get off the top, of the paint. I thought.

If you have ever had this happen then you will know how messy it is to remove that skin. Of course, you must remove the skin before stirring or you will end up with lumps in the paint.

"How do I store a can of paint so that when I open the can there will be no skin on the surface?" I asked a painter friend, many years ago.

"When you are finished painting put the lid on securely, turn the can upside down, and put it on the shelf. Next time you open it, and look in, you won't see a skin on top," was his answer.

He told me it was what he did all the time, and that it worked very well. What a pile of hockey pucks that was!

I stored a can of paint that way–once. I found, upon opening it, my friend was absolutely right, there was no visible skin on the surface of the paint. When I started to stir it, however, I found the skin floating up to the top from the bottom of the tin.

The theory was this. Upon turning the tin upside down, to store it, the air was no longer at the lid end of the tin because that end was the bottom of the tin. The bottom was now the top, and the air there would dry the surface out so a skin formed. When I turned the can over the skin started floating to the top.

When I took the lid off I could not see the skin so I started stirring. I was inexperienced in those days and I used a screwdriver to stir the paint; I know better now. The screwdriver broke the skin into chunks and I had just invented the first textured paint. This was not an acceptable solution.

I decided to find a way to solve this problem. After much thought I came to this conclusion, if there was a way to keep the air, in the tin, from coming in contact with the paint surface a skin would not form. Keeping this in mind I made my own, removable, skin for the surface. In the '50s we did not have polyethylene plastic so I used a piece of wax paper. I set the tin on a piece of wax paper and cut a circle out of the paper the size of the tin. I put the circle of wax paper on the surface of the paint, smoothing it out so it was in contact with the entire surface. When I opened the tin months later, and removed the wax paper, there was no skin on the paint-surface to make a mess. Today, I use a piece of a plastic bag cut in a circle the size of the tin. If it is placed on the top of the paint, it stays skin-free for months and months. When you are ready to paint, just pinch the poly in the middle and pull it out of the tin. For your own comfort I suggest you put a note on top of the paint can saying, "Do not shake until after removing poly skin". If you shake the tin with the plastic still in there you will have the poly skin down in the paint and it will be a mess to get it out.

Stop the Drip and Save Your Sanity and Money

"Did you hear that faucet dripping all night? It kept me awake and nearly drove me nuts," I grumbled to my wife at breakfast.

"Yes I did, and I asked you months ago to fix it. Will you do it now?" she came back.

There is nothing more irritating to hear, throughout the night, than drip… drip… drip… drip. When a faucet drips, it is not only irritating, it is a waste of natural resources and money. If you are on a water meter, you pay for water you did not use. If you pay for your sewer, based on the amount of water you use, then you have paid twice. If it happens to be hot water, you have paid a third time for water you did not use. It is time to spend a buck and fix the faucet.

There are **several** things to do when you replace a faucet and they **all** must be done at the same time or you will be going back into the faucet for more repairs.

First, **turn off the water!** This can be done, in most cases, by looking under the counter for the waterlines and the shut-off valves, then turning off the water to the faucet. This may seem an obvious statement to make but I know of a man who did not turn off the water; when he loosened the handle he had a geyser. Before he got the water turned off, the floor was covered, the ceiling was soaked and so was he. If there are no shut-off valves under the counter, then you must turn the water off at the main valve, where it comes into the house. Be careful here, the handle may stick and you do not want to force it. If you should break anything at that valve you could flood the house because, now, it can only be shut off by the city, out at the street.

With the water shut off, remove the little cap on the top of the faucet handle, the one with a "C" or an "H" on it, or a red or blue dot. A little, pointed knife will do the trick. You will see a bolt, which must be unscrewed. These bolts are generally made of a soft brass and can be damaged easily, so be careful. If the bolt does not come loose easily put a few drops of penetrating oil in the little well, and replace the cap and let stand for a few days.

Sometimes you will see a whitish-blue substance over the bolt. This is a collection of lime or salt. If it is soft just scrape it away. If it is hard and you cannot get to the bolt then fill the well with vinegar, put the cap back on, and let it stand for a week. Here is a note to the women readers: this is not a male ploy to avoid doing the work right now. The vinegar must be allowed to dissolve, or at least soften, the lime deposit.

When you remove the cap in a week the white material should be soft and can be scraped aside. Once the bolt has been removed the handle should come off readily. Once again, this may not be as easy as it sounds, be careful. Do not hammer the handle as it may be made of white metal or plastic and could break. Even, upwards pressure should get it off. If the handle does not come off, then buy or borrow a handle-puller. This little tool is invaluable. You will see how it works once you have one in your hands.

When the handle is off you are now facing the top of the cartridge. There is a large nut holding this cartridge in place. Loosen the nut: you will find it is part of the cartridge and the whole thing will lift out easily. Under this nut is a very thin washer, in some cases, made of fiber. This washer will likely disintegrate when you remove the cartridge. It must be replaced when you replace the cartridge in the faucet body. For replacement you should buy the plastic washers, which last much longer. (If you do not replace this washer you will have a water leak, coming out from under the handle, when you re-assemble it and turn the water back on again.) On the end of the cartridge is another washer, the one causing the problem. Just replace the washer, but you **must** use the proper size and configuration of washer. You may want to take the washer and the o-ring, which you will find shortly, to the hardware store, to match to the new ones.

While the cartridge is out check the seat inside the faucet. This is down at the bottom of the faucet-body. It can be felt by inserting the little finger into the faucet and running it around the seat. (Do not **force** your finger into the hole you could be wearing the faucet for a while.) If it is smooth, then leave it alone. If it is rough, it is time to replace it. The roughness is likely the cause of the damaged washer. There is a seat-removal tool that you can put down into the faucet to unthread the seat. This tool is available at most hardware stores or building centres.

You are not finished yet. The cartridge will come apart into two pieces: just unscrew the one from inside the other. Now, you have exposed the "O" ring. The "O" ring is another washer, which keeps the water from coming up around the cartridge and out around the handle. Replace this while you are at it. It is now time to reassemble the faucet and turn on the water.

There is an easier way, and a little more expensive of course. When you have the cartridge out, and you have replaced the seat, you can replace the whole cartridge, and the faucet is brand new.

In the case of the washerless faucet the only way to repair it is to replace the cartridge and that can be done quite easily. Many manufacturers guarantee their faucets and parts for life. If you have one of these you might just get a new cartridge free-of-charge. Check into it at your dealers. Good luck.

Use Bread When Soldering

I learned a couple of valuable lessons one Sunday evening when I was building a bathroom:

1) Do not do plumbing Sunday evening–or any evening for that matter.

2) Always keep some bread handy when you are soldering waterlines.

If you work all weekend on plumbing, and work well into the evening on Sunday, you will run into trouble with the plumbing: one of Hammar's Plumbing Laws.

I worked for several days installing some copper waterlines, for the new bathroom off the family room. The soldering went well until I was ready to cap off the vanity faucet lines and turn the water back on for the night. This was about 10 p.m. Sunday evening… no plumbing stores open then. The solder would not take on the one cap and it leaked. I could not turn the water back on until I had the cap tightly installed. That meant we would not be able to use the sinks or the toilets until Monday, when I could find out how to solve the problem.

Reluctantly, I called my brother-in-law. With his construction experience I was sure he would know what to do. He had to get out of bed and come over; not a happy camper was he.

"Get me a piece of bread," was the first thing he said.

"You can eat when the job is done," I objected. In those days he was just a growing young man and ate all the time.

"I need the bread to get the job done."

This was when I learned you could not solder a joint if there is water in the line, no matter how little. You see, the line was not tipped downward so the excess water would run out. This meant there was some water lying in the line. Water in the line absorbs the heat from the torch and the pipe does not get hot enough to melt the solder. He tore chunks out of the centre of the slice of bread and stuffed it into the pipe, and then with a long screwdriver he pushed it as far back into the pipe as he could. The torch was then applied to the pipe and the solder melted and sealed the cap to the end of the line. Now, to show you how tired and frustrated I was, I asked how I was going to get the #$@%&*$#@ (more shop talk) bread out of the line.

"Simple. When you install the faucets and turn them on the water will dissolve the bread and it will come out of the faucet."

How stupid can I be? I thought.

Chapter 4

The New House

With the many lessons learned through the years in the lumber business and a variety of how-to projects, this "all-thumbs" handyman turned his skills and attention to the construction of his own home, a tri-level house. A tri-level house is built with a centre dividing-wall as the main bearing partition. And the building of this house would build character and produce more than its share of bruises and mistakes.

Father Takes a Pratt Fall

In the very early sixties, my wife and I built our first house, and my late father kindly offered to help. I was a little dubious about this as my father was definitely not a handyman. He was a good salesman, public speaker, manager, businessman and negotiator. But a handyman? No way. I used to describe my father's handyman skills as, "He didn't even know which end of the hammer to use to apply paint." He was not quite that bad but close.

When he first came on the job he said, "Son, you are the boss and I'll do as you say."

Now that was something. He had never listened to me any time before so why would he start now? Do not get me wrong, I loved my father very much and I respected his business skills, but two of his non-skills, were not listening and not taking orders. However, he did listen and did follow most of my instructions and later confessed he had learned a great deal in the process.

Once, early in the "adventure" as he called it, we were setting the first-floor joists in place on the foundation. If you have never done this then I will explain. But, if you have, you will be way ahead of me on this story. A 2 X 6, called the mud sill, is bolted on the flat, to the top of the foundation. We "toe-nailed" 2 X 12 joists to the plate, and put in "bridging" as we went, pieces of 2 X 2 between the joists, to strengthen and hold the joists in place. Father was working from a ladder, which was standing on the dirt floor of the basement. I was working from above him on top of the joists. I nailed a 1 X 6 across the joists as I went, and I worked from this, nailing in the bridging.

"Dad, would you please bring me another bundle of bridging, from beside the saw table there in the basement?"

He turned and began to walk down the ladder. Notice I said, "walk down the ladder" not "climb down the ladder"–most significant in this case. He started down the ladder, the way you would walk down a set of stairs, and used a joist, which was loose and not attached with bridging yet, as a handrail, not thinking of course.

"Don't hang on to that……" I started to yell.

Too late. The joist rolled over and father fell from the ladder to the basement floor, some 6 or 7 feet below. Fortunately, the joist did not fall on top of him. He did fall on some concrete blocks, and broke two ribs, sprained his knee, and knocked the wind out of himself. He was not unconscious but close to it.

I was into the basement almost as fast as he was. Needless to say, he was off the job for several weeks nursing his injuries and wounded pride. When he came back he promised to obey **all** safety regulations. I learned from this accident as well: keep the work area clean.

His job, for several weeks after, was to clean up after the workers or before they arrived on the job site. The construction site was as clean as any finished home and maybe even neater. I know this has not been a fun story but I feel it is one, which must be told. **Be careful!**

The building of this house was an experience for both my wife and me. We learned to take the disappointments with the successes.

Many of the stories in this book come from what we learned during the construction of this house.

It Never Rains But it Pours

It has been said, "it never rains but that it pours", it certainly was true during the first two weeks of the framing of the house. I had managed, with the help of my wife, her uncle, her brother and my father, to put the joists and sub-floor in place, and cover it with tarpaper. A friend, who had a lot of experience in building, offered to take a week's holiday and come to work for me. I paid him for his help and we got a lot of the framing done on the first level.

On Monday, Jack arrived at 8 a.m. and my wife and I were there ready to start. It was pouring rain, coming down in buckets. Fortunately, as I said earlier, we had covered the sub floor with tarpaper, in anticipation of wet weather. After all, it was September when that kind of weather is common in southern Ontario. My wife spent the next week in the gloomy basement, with a 300-watt bulb hanging from the ceiling, cutting studs to size. (At least she was dry.) In those days there were no precut-studs. Jack and I worked above her in the rain. I followed his directions and learned. We had the first floor framed and the ceiling joists in place in a few days. The sub-floor for the second level went on quickly. By the end of his week's holidays we were ready to frame the second floor.

After that my wife and I built the rest of the house with the help of my father, hobbling around with a sprained knee, and her brother, a teenager full of energy, but not able to do much on his own.

A Plumbing Problem–Not the Water Kind

We did very well, and soon we were ready to put the ceiling joists in place for the third level. Here, we ran into our first major construction problem. The centre wall was the main wall from which all floors were suspended. It ran from the basement dividing-wall to the ceiling joists of the third level. It was imperative that this bearing partition be perfectly plumb. We found, when we were ready to install the ceiling joists for the third level, the centre wall was not plumb.

"What are we going to do to plumb this wall?" father asked.

He expected me to have the answer, right off the top of my head.

"The two of us will use a 2 X 4 as a lever, and pry the wall into place. Dad, you put the level on the stud and let us know when it's plumb. Then we can nail the braces in place and get on with the job."

All this was to no avail.

"Let's try my car jack," father suggested.

Father had a 1960 Cadillac. One of those big old boats... heavy as can be. The jack must to be strong to lift it, we reasoned.

"Well that didn't work," I said.

"What now?" he asked.

The light went on in my head and I rushed down to my little Austin automobile–just a box on wheels–but in this box was a very tough towrope.

"What on earth are you going to do with that?" they asked in unison.

"Just watch," I replied.

We tied the rope to the top of the wall and we tried, with three of us pulling, to pull the wall into a plumb position. No luck.

Here is where good old-fashioned ingenuity came into play. The first of many unusual solutions to the problems we encountered, while building this house. Leaving one end tied to the top of the wall I threw the other end of the rope down to the ground where I tied it to the frame of my car.

"You're not... are you?" father asked in astonishment.

"You hold the level on the stud while I ease the car into gear and slowly pull, Dad."

I instructed my brother-in-law to whistle when it was plumb.

I know my father must have thought me crazy but I knew it would work. It worked like a charm. We had the walls plumbed in no time.

Here I should point out the difference between "plumb" and level". Something is level only when on the horizontal, but something is plumb when it is straight up and down. Hence the name of this segment, "A Plumbing Problem".

The plumbing problem was solved and we got on with the work.

In the days when we were building our house, the early 1960s, there was not much of a building code, at a local level. The mortgage companies had very strict building codes, therefore local governments did not see a need to have a building code, as well.

Mortgage companies inspected each and every house, for which they loaned money. The unfortunate thing, in our case, was the first inspection was at the time of the installation of the foundation footings, and the next not until after the roof was completed. This caused us a real problem.

I had not paid close enough attention to the code for the installation of the 2 X 6 mud sill on the top of the foundation wall. If you look at the top of the foundation of your house you will see the mud sill on top of the concrete wall. This is where the floor joists for the first floor sit on the foundation. All the weight of the house sits on this mud sill. The mortgage companies code said I was must put some "mortar" under the mud sill, before tightening the nuts on the foundation bolts. Mortar is a cement-based material. When you put it on top of the concrete wall then set the sill into it and tighten the bolts, it is supposed to keep drafts from coming under the sill. In the coming years we would see caulking used to replace mortar, because it is flexible and will stay in place. Later still, we see a foam sheet used as a draft stop. I was given an "infraction" on my inspection, for not having mortar under the mud sill. This meant I would receive no further money from the mortgage company, until I corrected the infraction. I could not pay for materials and labour, until the infraction was corrected. I had a big problem: how do I get mortar under the sill when a three-story house is sitting on it?

I went to the mortgage company to see the head inspector, for help.

"How am I supposed to get mortar under the sill now?" I asked him.

His answer, "I don't know, it's your problem. You could put a pry bar under the sill and pry it up enough to put mortar under the sill, I guess."

I saw red as I thought, *Now that is a bright thing to say why didn't I think of it. I'll go right home have a bowl of spinach and do that little job. I should be finished in about a 100 years.*

"Tell me, how am I supposed to lift a three story house up and put mortar under the mud-sill. That is an impossible task," I enquired.

"Well, you should have thought of that when you started the house," he said. "Is there anything else I can help you with?" he said with a foolish grin on his face.

I was tempted, but opted for a one word answer, "No!"

A really stupid little man, I thought.

Fortunately for me, I ran into a friendly inspector in the hall, one who used to buy materials from me at the lumberyard. I told him what his boss, the head inspector, had told me.

He laughed and said, "Why don't you go home, squeeze caulking into the crack between the sill and the wall, then smear mortar over the caulking, while it is still wet. Call me at my home when you've done this, then put in for a re-inspection. I'll pick up the inspection notice and pass it for you."

He continued, "It really did not matter if it was mortar or caulking, in the crack, between the sill and wall. All the mortgage company wanted was a draft stop, under the mud sill".

It passed. I got my mortgage draw. Another job well done, thanks to a quick thinking building inspector.

Not Just Drinks can be Spiked

Ever heard of a "spike" knot in a piece of wood? No? Well I had, having been in the lumber business for over 10 years. But I had never really thought about what a spike knot could do until I built this house. My brother-in-law, and I were cutting and installing the roof rafters. The roof had two different pitches on it, a low slope pitch on the north side, and a steep pitch, with long rafters, on the south side. Complicated cuts were required on both ends of each rafter because of these two pitches. The top end of a rafter is nailed to a "ridge" board. This board, in our case, was 8-inches wide, to accommodate the long, angled cut on the one rafter, and ran the full length of the roof. We worked late one evening on this project and did very well.

"Let's call it quits for tonight. We have half the rafters in place and we can finish tomorrow," I called up to my brother-in-law on the scaffold.

"Sounds good to me. I'll be right down. Can we go for a hamburg?"

Always thinking of his stomach that guy.

He swung down from the scaffold on one of the rafters and **bang**! There was a loud crack just like a gun going off. Scared the daylights out of us both. We thought one of the neighbours had finally tired of hearing us hammer and saw late into the evening, and decided to end our days. But it came from the ridge-end of the rafter, so we climbed up the scaffold and looked at the ridge board. There was a spike knot in the ridge board, running lengthwise, about 15-inches. The ridge board had cracked the whole 15-inches and then run to the end of the board another three to four feet. We both sat down and cried.

"There're three hours of work shot all to heck," I moaned.

"What happened?" he asked me.

I explained to him, "We'll have to tear all those rafters out and start again tomorrow."

"At least we learned tonight how to do the job quickly, and to look at our ridge board before we put it in place," he said.

Windows, Rain and Drywall

Once the framing was complete it was time to install the windows. Since I worked for a lumberyard that supplied many of the contractors in our area, I had the pick of quality materials. I chose high-quality windows for our home because they were the best on the market and never regretted that decision. What I did regret however, was not putting the flashing, or drip cap, on the windows when we installed them; I thought I could do it later. As you will see, next, this was a mistake.

"That about finishes the drywall in the dining room. So, let's get started on the south wall of the living room," I said to my brother-in-law.

Right about this time a very bad, blowing rainstorm erupted and the rain just pelted down. We went to the living room and started the south wall. The wall of that room was under a four foot overhang and the windows were protected from the storm. We finished the south living room wall and decided to quit for the day.

"What the heck happened here?" he asked.

There was water on the floor of the dinning room.

"I don't know, and look at the wall. It's soaked," I said.

Since we had not capped and flashed the dining room window, on the outside, the rain came in around the window, soaked the insulation, the drywall and the floor. Another repair job to do and a lesson learned.

Always flash and seal windows and doors–for that matter any opening in an outside wall–right after installation. Avoid a money and time consuming repair.

It seemed the drywall on the south wall of the dining room had more lessons to teach us, as you will soon see.

How to Patch a Hole in Drywall

"Lets get some 16-foot 2 X 4s up here for the long closet in Jim's room."

My brother-in-law handed them from the basement to me into the recroom and I slid them up onto the dining room floor.

Thud. Crash. Thump!

"What the heck is that?"

I looked and saw the drywall on the south dining room wall, which we had just replaced a week ago after the water problem, had been pierced by a 2 X 4.

"I just put a 2 X 4 through the drywall in the dining room," I sheepishly admitted.

The 2 X 4s were 16-foot and the dining room was only 15-foot. It was bound to happen.

The hole was quite a good size and it took a piece of drywall about one foot square to fix it. I cut a patch big enough to cover the hole, then drew a line around the patch on the wall and cut that out. Now, I can put the patch in place. Right? Noooooooo. The patch fell right through the hole, of course. This is when I learned to measure the hole, cut a patch larger, and bevel the edges, beveling towards the back making the patch smaller at the rear. I then cut the hole to the size of the back of the patch. Next, I beveled the edges of the drywall opening, so it was larger in front and smaller behind, and the patch slid into the hole smoothly and flush with the surface, but did not fall through. I buttered the edges of the hole with drywall-compound and put the patch in place, taped the joints and finished in the usual manner. Done! But progress was set back 24 hours.

Tiling the Kitchen Floor

"Son, you are at a place in the construction, where I can't be of any more help. I'll beg off for now," Father said to me, one Sunday afternoon.

The drywall was completed and the finishing stages were underway.

That evening the phone rang and when I answered, "Michael?"

It was my mother.

"Yes, Mom, what can I do for you this evening?"

"You're almost ready to put the tile on the kitchen and bathroom floor, aren't you?"

"Yes, I was going to start that on the weekend. Why?" I asked her.

"I haven't done much to help you with the house so I was wondering… could I lay the tile floors?"

"Have you ever done that kind of job before, Mom?"

"No, but I am not too old to learn."

"Well, if you're game I'd be glad of the help," was my answer.

I gave her instructions and showed her how. By the time the tiling was finished Mom was an expert.

Another Boo Boo

Speaking of the bathroom, I must tell you this story. It speaks volumes for the need to heed one's spouse. Are you listening guys? I know it is hard for most guys to admit they made a mistake, or just did not listen to their spouse. Well, I am admitting to both of those things, here and now. After the bathtub had been installed in the upper bathroom, of the new house, I had to put drywall on the walls around it. I took my boots off, so I could stand in the tub and not damage it.

My wife, asked, "Would it be a wise move to put some padding in the tub, just in case you dropped something? It wouldn't damage the tub then".

"Michael! Did you hear my suggestion? Put a pad in the tub," she urged, again… I ignored her, as before.

Well, wouldn't you know it! I dropped the hammer into the tub and a big chip came out of the enamel. Was my face red or what?

Forever after I would be reminded of my transgressions, every time I cleaned the tub or looked into it. The moral of this story is… guys, never be ashamed to take suggestions from your wife when doing a job. If it does not work out you can always blame her for the mess.

Son Jimmy and Drywall Compound

We called our son Jimmy, when he was little, and Jimmy was always into something. He was an inquisitive boy: loved to climb into, get onto and under things… always in a place he should not be. His nickname was, The Mouse.

"We've brought Jimmy to see what Mom and Dad are doing, at the new house," my mother said.

We were just applying the drywall compound, or mud as it is called, to the joints of the drywall, in the house. My mother and father had come for a visit, and to bring Jimmy to see us. They were looking after him, for the day, while we worked on the house.

We were doing the ceilings, and had rented scaffolding, to make it easier to reach the ceiling. It was at just the right height. Dad set Jimmy down on the floor, to run around, while we talked and showed them how much we had done that morning.

Next thing we knew Mom said, "Look at Jimmy, up on the scaffold."

He had climbed up and onto the platform, and stepped into the tub of wet drywall mud. Jimmy just stood there, ankle deep, with a big grin on his face. I wish I had taken his picture; it was priceless. Another mess, but it was easy to clean up.

Practicing Safety on the Job is a Must

One Sunday I was working at the house on my own high up on a scaffold. I learned, from what happened, that working alone up high or in a dangerous place is forbidden.

I was outside on the scaffold two and a half stories up, at roof level, installing the fascia on the rafter ends. I had put pieces of wood under the legs of the scaffold, so they would not sink into the ground and would remain stable. Unfortunately, I used only 1 X 8 wood under one leg, I should have used 2 X 8; that leg was on lower ground and needed leveling. I climbed up on the scaffold and was working along quite nicely when my father arrived.

"Hi, Michael. I came to give you a hand with the fascia," my father called out from the ground.

I walked over to the street side of the scaffold, to speak to him, and… you guessed it, the scaffold settled a bit, the piece of 1 X 8 cracked and the leg sank into the ground, and the scaffold tipped. I was a full two and a half stories up in the air. I grabbed the piece of fascia, which I had just nailed in place, and held on.

"Hang on son, I am coming," father said frantically.

He raced up stairs, put a rope around the frame of the scaffold and tied it off. I could have been killed. If the scaffold had continued on its way down I would have landed on the concrete sidewalk or on the road.

The lesson: stabilize the scaffold or ladder and tie it off to keep it from tipping or sliding away, when you are working up high like that, and do not work alone.

The Last New House Story... I Promise

It was two years, plus a month, before we moved into the "new" house. We had been living in a rented house while building, and had given our notice to vacate, 30 days earlier. I thought I would have the house in shape for us to move into by Thanksgiving Day, 1962, which was also Jimmy's birthday. I was a little short on my estimate, another 30 days would have been better.

I borrowed the one-ton flat-bed truck from work, and we asked one of my wife's brothers, and his wife to help us move.

I had not finished building the stairs and installing them. So there I was, in the living room, building stairs, while the furniture was being put into the dining room.

"Do you think you'll be finished in time for us to put the bed-room furniture upstairs tonight?" My wife asked.

"I don't know; I am working as fast as I can. Don't want to make any mistakes."

I was frantically building, my first set of stairs ever, and all around me people were moving stuff into the house. I finished the stairs to the first upper floor by suppertime. We installed them and moved furniture up them all evening. The hardwood floors had not been installed, yet, so we lived on the 1 X 6 sub floor for some time.

I learned many lessons, while building this house. I learned that I could problem-solve while in the middle of a job, a skill first taught to me by my Grandpa Mac.

This skill was of great use years later, when I hosted my-call-in, home-handyman, radio-show. It was a problem a minute some-times. Most times the problems were ones I had solved before but they were put to me in different ways. Sometimes, the problem was unique and that is where Grandpa Mac's teachings came in handy. I will always be grateful to him for the things he taught me.

For more about my Grandpa Mac see page 143

Chapter 5

My DIY Misadventures
Words that make your skin crawl

Although I am considered to be a "professional" handyman there are still things I do not like to do. Why? Because they are hard, dirty or I find them difficult to do, or maybe all of the above. And my wife comes up with at least one of these projects a year. You guys will know what I am speaking of when I say there are phrases in my wife's vocabulary, which make me cringe.

"I'm really happy with the look of the house, it is so comfortable… but…"

Words that make your skin crawl. Right guys?

Translated: It is time for us to go to war again, so get on your battle dress and bring out your best objections, but you know you can not win.

Rob's Problem and I'm All Wet Here

One of my best friends; let us call him Rob, was very good at his career, but he was, in those days, not very handy with a hammer and saw. He and his wife bought a house for their family. It had been built by one of the city's better contractors. They assumed, as most people would, that the contractor used the best materials and his most experienced craftsmen. The following story will prove that assumption incorrect.

"I have to put up a ceiling in the office downstairs. I've never put one up before, can you give me any advice?"

"Have you been bushwhacked into putting up that ceiling? I thought there was a perfectly good drywall ceiling in that room?"

"There is, but it's not good enough. She wants a tile ceiling there… something about looking more pleasing or some such nonsense." So, I agreed to help him install an acoustic ceiling.

When you are considered a home improvement expert people expect you know about everything and how to do everything around a house. They also assume you do not make mistakes. Guess what? I do not know everything and, yes, I do make mistakes. How do you think I became an expert? One of my mistakes follows, but it really was not my fault, honest.

"Rob, since we can't see where the joists are I'll use the stud sensor to find them and the ones we can't find, we locate by measuring from the ones we have found."

When I worked with Rob I always tried to teach him what I was doing. He wanted to learn how to do stuff around the house. When he first foolishly expressed an interest in home improvements I advised him to be a klutz so he would not have to work around the house. Advice he ignored; I am sorry to say.

We found all the ceiling joists without a problem. We took down the light fixture in the centre of the room. Now we could actually see the joist next to the octagon-box; and that helped give us a fix. But there was something we did not take into consideration, and should not have had to, as you will see.

"When you put up ceiling tile you start strapping, with the 1 X 3 straps, from the centre of the room. This means your tile will end up being the same size on either side next to the wall," were my instructions.

"That seems reasonable. How are we going to handle the fixture in the middle of the room?" was his question.

"I'll simply put pieces of strapping around the octagon-box and the tile will staple nicely in place."

Rob and I started putting up the 1 X 3 strapping. We put in just a few nails to hold the strapping and then, while he went back to finish the nailing, I went to work on the small pieces around the light fixture. Here is where the trouble began and I soon found out I was "all wet" about this job.

I measured the pieces required, and nailed one in place. Next, I nailed the other piece in place on the opposite side of the box. ZAP! No, I did not hit a hot wire-I hit the hot water line.

"Holy cow, water!" I screamed.

"Where?" Rob said.

"Beside the electrical box; right up against it. Who in their right mind would put a water line against an electrical box?"

Well, some idiot did; and I knew who; the contractor! The hot water started to spray out over me. So, like an inexperienced do-it-yourselfer I pulled the nail out of the hole and the water shot out even faster.

"Rob, shut off the water at the main line."

"I don't know where it is."

"Well, find it, or we're going to be flooded here."

I knew I would need a shower after an evening's work–but, now, with my clothes on?

Rob and his family had moved into the house a year or so earlier and up to now there had been no need to shut off the water.

Here is another tip for you: when you move into a new house find the fuse box and the main water shut-off right away. Emergencies do happen.

Like the little boy who put his finger into the dike, I put my finger up against the hole to stop the leak. Ouch!

"That's hot water, stupid," my finger told me.

I jumped down and Rob and I got one of the kids' small inflatable swimming pools from the backyard. We put it on a table under the leak to catch the water so the basement would not flood, and then scurried around like rats trying to escape a sinking ship. My reputation was in jeopardy.

Trying to find the main shut off was like trying to find a needle in a haystack. It was not where one would expect it should be, on the water line coming into the house from the front street, just inside the front foundation wall. Since the contractor was going to live in the house he put the shut off in an unusual place convenient for him. The shut off was in a very small space behind the furnace, where only a small person could reach it. Thank goodness I got to it in time... the pool was filling up fast!

Now here is where I did not think. If I had just shut off the intake line to the hot water tank the water from the tank would have stopped flowing. I was lucky, the water coming out of the line could have been even hotter; I could have been seriously burnt. Another lesson learned and my expertise grew.

With all the excitement and running around, I had not noticed I was all wet.

Since Rob did not have the tools or equipment to fix the copper line I called my son, Jim, for help, and to bring his tools along with some warm, dry clothes for me. This was definitely not one of my better days as an "expert". I had to agree with one person's definition of the word "eXpert". "X" is an unknown quantity and a spurt is a little drip under pressure. Enough said.

To answer your question; yes we did get the room cleaned up, dried and the ceiling finished.

We'll Just Spend a Few Bucks

"Let's make this place a little brighter and more up to date. You know, a little paper here, a little paint there. And, while we're at it let's throw some new vinyl down in the kitchen. We'll just spend a few bucks to make the old place new again," my wife said.

Sound familiar?

You and I, being practical males, know that a few bucks are just the beginning. Those few bucks are the down payment on weeks of pain and agony. Along with this renovation frenzy, comes the laying of carpet. This happened in our house one year.

I was heading off to perform at a home show. Wouldn't you know, that was the day the carpet installers chose to arrive? Coincidence or accident–maybe planned? Who knows?

Years later I was to pay the price for my wife's misunderstanding, if that is what it was, of my instructions for the installation of the carpet.

"When the carpet installers arrive, please remind them we do not want the carpet glued in place over the old vinyl tile."

"But won't it move?"

"Remember, we asked them about that and they assured us it would stay put. If we ever have to take the carpet up I don't want to wrestle with a glued carpet."

I thought my instructions were quite explicit. Do not let them glue it in place. What is so mysterious about the words **do not**? I always thought **do not** meant **do not do it** but, obviously, she could be convinced otherwise.

When I came home from the show the carpet had been installed, using glue of the toughest kind, as I was to find out many years later.

"They said it had to be glued in place," she told me.

"But, when we bought it we asked them if it could be put down 'loose lay'. Their answer was 'yes' so, why did they glue it?"

I called the installers and one said, "Sorry, but I guess you will have to live with it now.

My reaction is not printable so I will go on with the rest of the story.

Many years later we put in new kitchen cabinets. Before having them installed I removed the old kitchen cabinets and used them in the basement.

With the cabinets out, I started to take the carpet up, following the method I had given so many people over the years. I got out the square-mouthed spade and started to try to lift the carpet at a corner. Pry, pry, pry: Nothing. The top layer came up but not the foam pad under it. Not to worry, I will use some solvent to dissolve the glue. But, no way would this work. I tried scraping and it still would not come. (There are products on the market, today, to do this. Ask your flooring retailer what they carry for this job.)

The vinyl tile and the carpet's foam back would not come away from the plywood underlay. As I scraped and pulled, bits and pieces of all three came up. More frustration, anger and lots of shop-talk. The air was positively blue with shop-talk.

Finally I resorted to lifting the plywood underlay, tile and foam pad along with it. Do you know how many nails are in a sheet of underlay? Answer: approximately 288, &*%$#@ nails. Today, they use a stapling machine but then they used ringed nails. This type of nail was meant to go in easily but stay forever. In prying up the plywood many of the nails broke off at the head, leaving stubs sticking out. When the plywood underlay was up I had to crawl around on my knees, sometimes kneeling on a blasted nail-stub, with a pair of pliers I pulled the stubs out, before new plywood underlay could be installed.

If my wife had been within hearing range she would have known why I said, "**do not**" let them glue the carpet down."

So much for communication.

Painting Over Varnished Wood and the Chip-Tip

This topic really makes the hackles stand up on the back of my neck. Grandpa Mac brought me up to love natural-looking wood in all its beauty and it really bothers me when someone wants to paint it.

To paint wood or not to paint wood, that is the question. In our home, the question was debated: is it nobler to paint natural, beautiful wood or is it a sin to paint natural, beautiful wood? Being brought up by a grandfather who loved the smell, look and feel of natural wood I am of the opinion it is a sin of the first degree to paint it. In my mind a clear protective coating is the only thing to put on natural wood.

My wife is of the opinion that, if trees without grain could be grown, then she would not have to paint natural wood.

What she objects to is the "weird" configuration of grains. Now, I thought that was the beauty of natural wood. Some people have a weird sense of what looks beautiful. This comes at a time when...

"It is being done by all of the decorators," she says.

Decorators are those people who are supposed to know the correct thing to do. Now I ask you who, in their right mind, would paint over walnut, mahogany, birch, cherry and other exotic woods? I guess if we answer that question correctly, we would have to say decorators are not in their right minds, at least not in my opinion. I will get off my soapbox now and give you some tips for painting over varnished or clear-finished surfaces, if you really have too.

Painting over a previously clear-finished surface is not a good idea, without the proper preparation, as the paint can chip easily since it will not likely bond well to the clear finish. Ideally, sanding the surface or removing the clear finish with chemical remover is best. However, there are products on the market made to help. One such product is liquid sandpaper. Because sanding fancy trim, spindles and such is difficult, liquid sandpaper can be applied to the varnished surface. It flattens the surface and provides a grip for the primer. Yes, you must prime first. Some paint manufacturers now make primers, which are meant to bond to shiny surfaces, even glass. If you use this type of primer they say no sanding of the surface is necessary.

According to paint manufacturers, when you apply paint, apply it in thin coats.

Have you ever-noticed in older houses how easily the paint chips on the door trim or baseboard? Generally, painting layer upon layer of paint causes this. Too many layers of paint on the surface and it might become brittle. Bump it and, pop, off comes some of the paint. You may also notice it chips right down to the old varnish; which is an indication of improper preparation of the original surface.

As I have said before and will likely say again, "Preparation or the foundation laid before the job is started is the most important part of the job."

Always Keep the Eaves Clean!

"Practice what you preach", someone once said.

If I had, I would not be telling this story.

My wife and I were putting an addition on our house. Our neighbour Stanley was helping me finish the installation of the roofing and the skylights.

From the roof we could see the black foreboding sky over Buffalo, New York, to the southeast–the capital for bad weather in that part of the world; sorry Buffalo. It was late September. Lightning flashed in the distance and arctic-cold air held a promise of rain.

The final, rough outside work had to be finished today. We worked frantically to complete the installation of two skylights before the rain came.

We kept an eye on the sky to the southeast. It got darker and darker. and the storm rolled towards us. We were dancing as fast as we could, but the music would not play any faster. The skylights went in easily and the last of the roofing went into place–just in time.

Finally, I said to Stanley, "You better head for home."

I finished up and went inside and my wife had a hot cup of tea ready for me. We went to the front door and stood looking out as the rain and lightening came and the wind blew.

"Boy, I thank my lucky stars we're finished," I commented.

As we stood there my wife said, "You didn't clean the eaves-troughs this fall, did you dear?"

You guys know the tone of voice, which accompanies that kind of question.

"No, because we were too busy on the addition," I replied.

"Well, you better look out there, and do something about the Niagara Falls pouring off our roof."

Sure enough the downspout was plugged and the rainwater was flowing out of the trough and into the garden.

"I'll clean it out when the rain stops".

"I just planted all the bulbs for spring this afternoon and now they're floating out into the yard. I think now would be a good time to do something about that waterfall, before everything has to be replanted."

"Okay! Okay! I'll do it now."

I put on my rain jacket and got the stepladder out. The rain had let up quite a bit so I was in no danger of drowning.

Safety when setting up a ladder is a must. Always be sure the legs are on solid ground. I made sure, or so I thought, that the ladder was solid and firm. I climbed up to the edge of the roof.

Picture this if you will. I was at the corner of the house. The eavestrough ran along the fascia board, to my left, and the fascia of the gable ran up to the ridge, on my right.

I hung onto the gable fascia, with my right hand, to steady myself, and started pulling the leaves out of the eavestrough with my left hand. Everything was going, pardon the pun, swimmingly, when the one leg of the ladder sank into the wet soil, in the garden, and the ladder fell over. I was dangling from the eavestrough, with my left hand, and the gable fascia with my right hand. The water was still running over the end of the trough, and now down inside my rainjacket sleeve, under the front of my T-shirt, and the front of my jeans, and out my left pant leg.

With a cup of tea in her one hand, and my glasses in her other, my wife just stood there laughing. I did not think it was funny.

"Come on, help me!" I pleaded.

What a dilemma. Dropping to the ground was not an option. The fallen ladder lay at an angle directly below me. With my short legs serious damage would have been done to me if I did drop to the ground, straddling the ladder. I could not pull myself up onto the roof and my wife would not stop laughing. There I was, fit to be tied–or badly injured.

How did it end? She finally put down the tea and my glasses and came to my rescue, but she was still laughing, and is probably still laughing to this day.

The Law of Water Flow

"Michael! Look what's happening in your workshop."

"Oh my gosh! Where'd the water come from?"

There was a river of water running through my workshop to the drain in the centre of the basement floor. I traced the flow's origin: the corner, where the concrete floor met two concrete block walls.

This particular leak taught me a great lesson about leaky basements. I realized that water is lazy–much like me, I guess. As water flows it finds the path of least resistance, and then takes that path. I did not think much about the Law-of-Water- Flow until we had that leak in the block basement.

In 1960 we built a house with a block basement. I would never do that again, and you will see why.

When the contractor poured the concrete floor in the garage he did not fill the tops of the blocks with concrete first, as he should have. The floor was poured right out over the tops of these blocks, and flush with the outside of the block wall. You might think the concrete for the floor would have filled the blocks as it was poured, but it did not. The next spring when we had rain the water ran down the driveway to the garage. There was a slight downward slope to the driveway, with a drain in the garage to catch water which might run in under the door. (Today in many areas, the code says there must be a drain outside the garage as well, to catch water flowing down the driveway.) The water went under the concrete floor, and into the hollow block. The block acted as a pipeline right down into the basement, and into my workshop.

We were on very sandy soil and the water brought some sandy silt in with it. So, the wall was not only wet but also dirty. Before I knew where the water was actually getting into the block, to save money, and because I am inherently lazy, I decided to waterproof the bottom row of blocks only. I used a very good waterproofer, a product I sold in the lumberyard in which I worked. It worked, and very well.

During the next big rain, the bottom row of blocks filled up from above and the water came in over their tops. I waterproofed the next row of blocks. The next time it rained, the water built up and ran over the top of those blocks. Now, I was getting mad. So, I waterproofed to the top of the third row of blocks. The water could not build up to the top of them so it ran around the corner into the sidewall and leaked into the shop again.

This is when I realized that water followed the line of least resistance. I really should have looked for the cause of the water getting into the blocks and fixed that problem. This I did… eventually. If I had found the cause, earlier, I would not have had to use waterproofing.

I called the contractor, and he came over, took one look and said– profoundly, "Oops!"

Well, I was aghast at that wise utterance.

"I made a mistake. I'll correct it," was his promise.

He did correct the problem by caulking between the concrete driveway and the concrete garage floor. (See Handy Tip #19 Chapter 11 page 133 for method used.)

I suggest here, if you have a leak in your basement look for the source and correct the problem, and the water flow will stop. It might simply be a matter of redirecting the downspouts.

Speaking of Downspouts, Here is Another Water Story

Downspouts were put on your eavestrough for a reason: to conduct the water from your eavestrough down to the ground. Hence, "down" spouts. Now, everyone knew that, did they not? It is necessary to direct the water away from the foundation– along way away from the foundation. If you allow the water from your roof to drain onto the ground next to your foundation you will have a leak in the basement. This is a certainty… but it may not always be through the basement wall, as you will see later. It is necessary to direct the water flow away from the house towards the yard. Rainwater directed out to the yard is good for the grass anyway.

There are many ways to do this; the most common way is to install an elbow on the end of the downspout, and then connect a ten-foot piece of downspout to it, directing the water out onto the lawn. The only problem with this is the horizontal downspouts have to be disconnected when you cut the grass, and then put back after. This is where problems sometimes arise.

One Saturday our son cut the grass and took the horizontal downspouts off, and then forgot to put them back on again. Let me say here that I have done this, as well. It is easy to do.

As a reward for a hard days work I took the family out to the movies that night: Sound of Music, I think it was, complete with popcorn, pop, the whole nine yards. While we were in the theatre, it rained. I mean thunder, lightning and about ten inches of water. At least it seemed like that much.

I may have exaggerated there just a little, but it rained so much in fact, that the theatre parking lot flooded. I bet you can see what is coming here: the foundation leaked, right? A good guess, but... wrong. The water from the roof ran out onto the lawn next to the house foundation. It came so fast, and in such volume, there was no time for it to soak into the ground. It ran along beside the foundation and into the window-well.

Today, in most areas, window-wells must drain into the weeping tile around the foundation. When our house was built in the late 60s this was not the code. The window-well filled with water and the water found its way into the house around the window. The windows were steel and did not fit well, which was common for the time. Although I bought the best wooden windows for the rest of the house, steel basement windows was all that was available to me then.

When we came home I went to the basement because I could hear water running and splashing.

"What the Sam Hill is happening?"

"Is it the hot water tank?" my wife asked.

I, too, thought the water tank had sprung a leak. That happened once but that is another story.

My desk was situated in the basement under the window

"Look at that! Like the little boy in the fountain in Rome the water is peeing in a stream right onto my desk. Oh, my gosh, what a mess!"

There was water everywhere you looked. Everything on my desk, in my desk and under my desk was wet. Not just wet, but soaked. It took the rest of the evening to clean up the mess, and another three days to get everything dry. We all remembered, after that, to put the horizontal downspouts back on after cutting the grass–at least for the next few weeks.

Eventually, I corrected that problem. I moved! No, not really. I ran a flexible, 4-inch, drain line from the downspout under the lawn to the lower part of the back yard. No more horizontal downspouts to forget to put back in place. Our house was on sandy soil so the water soaked into the ground quickly, and the grass grew better at the end of the downspout drain.

Chapter 6

Using Your Head for More than a Hat Rack!

Grandpa Mac would say, when I needed a solution to a problem: "Michael, my boy, use your head for more than a hat rack".

To this day when I am stumped for a solution, I hear that phrase in my head. I've found solutions, many times, by just sitting back and thinking. Other times, I have walked away from the problem and let my thoughts "percolate" in my head until the solution, or at least a direction to the solution, came.

Rodan's sculpture, "The Thinker", says more about the problem-solving process than most of us realize. I am a person who likes to just jump in and get the problem solved and the job done. Many times, when I have done this, I have gotten into more trouble. Most of the time, you can not just rush in because the mere action of rushing messes things up. The following stories might help you see the wisdom of thinking about problems and lead you to a solution or two.

Dust from Sanding or the Mysteries of a Tack Cloth

"I'm going to put a finish on the coffee-table top this afternoon, while you are out. I hope to have it finished by the time you get back," I announced to my wife.

"Thanks, dear. I know it will look great. Remember on this one I want a high smooth shine," she reminded me.

"Right you are, high smooth shine it'll be," I assured her.

Here is the way it goes when you are finishing a surface. You sand a piece of wood, in preparation for finishing, and you create a wood finisher's worst enemy. It is a four-letter word, D-U-S-T.

If you do not remove the dust completely or properly from a piece of material to be finished, you will end up with a nonskid surface, one which is pebbly and rough. This is probably not the finish you planned. Remember, sanding dust is made up of very fine particles of wood. The wood dust that gets onto the finish is embedded in it, and only stripping or more sanding, down to the bare wood, will clean it up.

The fine dust created when sanding, could be vacuumed or brushed off the project, but you will find much of it stays in the air. Yes, even vacuuming will put dust into the air. By the way, when was the last time you replaced the filter in your shop vacuum?

"A filter in the shop vacuum?" I hear you ask.

Yes, there is a filter in the shop vacuum and it must be kept clean. Clean it on a regular basis or replace it often. If you do not clean or replace the filter regularly you could be drawing dust in one end and blowing it out the exhaust end.

A Michael Hammar truism: sanding dust will stay in the air until you put the first coat of finish on the project.

Then like a magnet-zap! It finds its way to the wet surface, giving you a rough and bumpy finish.

The only way, I have found, to avoid the rough surface is to use a tack cloth, to remove the dust. You can buy these for a few dollars, in hardware stores, or you can make one yourself. Traditionally a tack cloth is a piece of cheesecloth, dipped in a finish and wrung almost dry, and stored in a can or plastic bag. This makes the cloth sticky or tacky, hence the name tack cloth. It is easier, and I think better, to buy the cloth; making your own with finish, is quite messy. You can end up with finish from stem to gudgeon, after wringing out the cloth.

I have found a better way to make a tack cloth, using a chamois and water, which is not a messy process. I bought a package of manufactured chamois cloths at a home show. The material absorbs water easily, but when you wring it out is only damp, not wet. Now you have a tack cloth that is inexpensive and will not dry out and have to be thrown away. When it is dry, just wet it again and wring it out.

To use a tack cloth, simply, wipe it over the surface to pick up the fine dust. The dust will not float into the air, as it will when a dry cloth is used. When you use the chamois cloth, which is barely damp, it will not leave a wet surface behind. If you use an old duster, and wet it, you will find the surface of the project will be wet. Since you cannot wring all of the water out of the old duster, a film of moisture is left behind on your project, and the grain in the wood will rise, making it necessary to sand again. To prove this to yourself, wet a dishcloth or old duster, wring it out as dry as you can. Now wipe your kitchen counter top with the cloth. See, you left water, which now must be dried off the kitchen counter top.

Before we leave this subject, I would like to tell a dust-and-wet-finish story, which taught me several things.

One time, in my workshop, I was putting a clear-coat finish on a tabletop. I had used the tack cloth to take all dust from the tabletop, so I knew there was no dust on the top. I applied the finish evenly, then went upstairs to watch TV, a golf game, while the finish dried. When I went back to the shop several hours later the finish was dry, but it was not smooth as glass: it was as rough as sandpaper. Boy, did the shoptalk fly then. Thank goodness there was no one at home.

I could not figure out why, after cleaning the top with a tack cloth, there was dust imbedded in the finish. I went back upstairs wailing and wringing my hands, to let the problem percolate in my brain. A few hours later, I went back down to look at the tabletop, hoping against hope that the problem had solved itself. It had not. I wiped my hand over the top, and it came away with a little dust on it. The light went on, and the explanation came to mind. I was applying the finish in the workshop area in which I had done sanding, sawing and other dusty jobs. I looked up; there was very fine dust on the shop ceiling–the subfloor and joists above. When I walked over the floor to the TV upstairs, I vibrated the subfloor, the ceiling of my shop, and dust fell off onto the wet tabletop. If your shop is like mine and most others you will have to cover the ceiling, temporarily at least, with cardboard or plastic.

But the solution is simple: do your finishing in a dust-free environment.

Of course, I had to use a finish remover to take the rough finish off the table and start again. No amount of sanding, unless I had sanded to the bare wood, could have made that surface smooth and mark-free.

Wobbly Chair Legs

My three-year-old granddaughter was sitting in a pressed-back highchair, wiggling around, as most little kids do at that age.

"Look, that chair is going to fall apart. The leg is loose in the seat," my wife exclaimed.

"I never noticed that before. I better take it to the shop and fix it soon," was my response.

"Like right now, I think," she declared.

So, we lifted our granddaughter out of the chair, and took it into my workshop for immediate repair.

I remembered what Grandpa Mac told me to do in cases like this.

"Michael, take the fine-toothed mitre saw and cut a short slit in the end of the leg. Whittle a hardwood wedge, just long enough and narrow enough, to fit in that slit. Scrape all the old glue off the leg and out of the socket in the seat, new glue will not stick to old glue. Put glue on the wedge and put the wedge into the slit then shove the leg back into the socket. Tap the leg into place and let dry. The wedge, as you drive it into the socket, pushes down into the leg and spreads the end of the leg. This makes a tight joint. But it will take some practice," Grandpa Mac instructed.

My attempts only gave me a split leg. I guess I made the cuts too small, the wedge too large, or maybe I should have cut across the grain and not with the grain. I do not know. In any event, I came up with a solution of my own, which I think is easier and faster, at least for the amateur. Sorry, Grandpa Mac, but that is the way it is.

Pull the leg out of the seat, if it is not already out. You will find there is hard glue on the end of the leg and in the hole in which the leg was inserted. As Grandpa Mac told me, the old glue must be removed. A sharp knife, chisel or sandpaper will do the trick. Once you have removed the glue, you will find the leg end is too small for the size of the hole in the seat. This occurred because, over the years as the chair wiggled the hole got larger. When you removed the glue the leg was slightly smaller and the hole slightly larger.

With my method I use short, narrow strips of cotton cloth soaked in glue.

To make the repair follow this procedure: Do a dry run first, to see how many strips of cotton are required. Put just enough strips over the end of the leg to make it fit snuggly when you tap it back into the seat.

Now, take the dry cotton strips off the end of the leg and, after putting some glue into a saucer, put the cotton strips into the glue. Make sure the glue saturates the cotton strips. If the glue is too thick it can be thinned with water, usually. Do not make it too thin but just thin enough to soak into the cotton. When the strips have been soaked remove them from the saucer, squeeze out the excess glue, by sliding the strips between your index finger and the middle finger. Now, place the strips over the end of the leg, building up the thicknesses. I always do a dry run first, to see how many strips of cotton are required. Put just enough strips on the leg end to make it a tight fit when it is tapped back into the hole in the seat. Of course, there will be bits of cloth sticking out from the hole beside the leg. These you will cut off with a sharp knife, before the glue dries. Now the leg is wedged in place, and with a glue wedge. No more wobbles from this chair. I have done this many times, and it has worked every time.

When you took the chair apart you undoubtedly removed the stretchers, the pieces connecting two legs. The stretchers must be put back and glued in place at the same time you replace the leg.

The tools and materials needed are: White or carpenter, glue, strips of old cotton cloth (material from an old shirt would work very well). The tools needed are a chisel or sharp knife, sandpaper, a small dish such as a saucer, and a rubber mallet.

Hanging a Picture Level

How many times have you hung a picture and found that it kept tilting to one side or the other? With only one nail in the wall it is difficult to hang any picture level, let alone keep it level. There is a way to keep pictures from tilting, and it is quite simple.

Think about how a picture is hung. There is a wire attached to the back of the frame, at each side. A nail is put into the wall, in an appropriate place, and the picture is hung by the wire. If there is just one nail in the wall the picture will slide off centre every time someone walks past, slams a door, or when a truck rumbles down the street. Use two nails placed in the wall on a horizontal line, about one quarter of the distance in from each edge of the frame. When the picture is hung it will not slide or tilt. The weight of the picture is distributed on both hangers and it cannot slide to one side or the other.

Here is another little tip, about pictures, which a late friend gave to me. Have you ever taken a picture down and found marks where the corners of the frame touched the wall?

"Pick up a package of those little round felt pad stick-on bumpers, the ones used on the corners of cabinet doors, to silence the sound of the closing door," she said. "Fasten them to the bottom corners of the frame and no more marks."

You guessed it; the pads touch the wall protecting it from damage. Good idea right?

A Dust Catcher when Drilling Holes

The following incident took place many, many years ago. The trick I learned that day I have used often ever since. I have shared this tip with thousands of people over the years but no one seems to know where it originated

"I would like to hang that new flower basket in the corner of the dining room. Would you be a good boy and put it up for me?" my wife asked.

"Yes, of course I would." What else could I say?

"Don't make a big dusty mess like you did the last time, please," was her request.

"But when I drill into plaster or drywall the fine dust flies everywhere," was my explanation for the mess.

Every time you drill a hole overhead the dust made by drilling floats down over everything. It goes up your nose, in your eyes and hair, all over your clothes, the furniture and the floor. You get the job done, but the cleanup takes you longer than the job. There is a way to keep the dust from taking over the room and your life.

I have used the vacuum and the attachment hose. While drilling, I have held the hose up by the ceiling, where I was drilling, and sucked up the dust. Unfortunately, as you probably already know, you need a hand to hold the drill, a hand to hold the hose and a hand to position the bit, this makes a total of three hands, count them. I do not know about you but I have only two.

"I just saw, on TV the other day, a method for catching the dust when drilling into a ceiling. Would you like to know what that method is?" my wife asked.

"Boy would I ever. Tell me please," I answered with enthusiasm.

"The guy said to use a paper cup, (today we would likely use a foam cup) drill a hole in the bottom the size of the shank of the drill bit. Put the bit through the hole and into the jaws of the chuck and tighten the chuck. Put the drill on the mark on the ceiling, push the cup up to the ceiling, and hold it in place and drill. All of the dust goes into the cup," she explained. "Neat eh?"

"I gotta see how that works," I responded.

Most of the time I have found it is necessary to cut the top of the cup off, so about two inches of the bit extends above the top of the cup.

The first time I did this my wife stood and watched. We were both pleased with the results, until I dropped the drill to my side, to come down the ladder. Yes, you guessed it; the dust was all over the floor, my pant-leg and the ladder. Big clean up. I have learned my lesson. Now, that is experience.

For a larger hole, such as one made by a hole-saw, use a margarine or yogurt container. Drill the hole in the bottom of the container, only the size of the drill shank not the hole saw. Slide the container over the shank end of the bit, put the shank into the drill's chuck, and drill the hole as above. It works every time. Next time you drill a hole in the ceiling use this method and you will be a hero–at least for an hour or two any way.

I have used this method while drilling a hole in a wall, as well. It is a bit harder to do, as you must be sure the cup is tight against the wall, but it does work.

Removing Black Scuff Marks from Floors

"Look at the black mark your shoes have made on the vinyl floor in the kitchen. I would like you to get rid of those shoes; they make such a mess. The marks are hard to clean off and I'm down on my knees scrubbing every week," my wife informed me.

I pointed to the mark, with the toe of the offending shoe, rubbing it across the mark, saying, "Is this the mark you mean?"

Amazingly, the toe of the shoe erased the part of the mark I had drawn it across. I did it again and again; the mark completely disappeared.

"Wow. Did you see that?" I exclaimed.

"Try it on the other marks and see what happens," she said.

I did, and was amazed at how easily it worked. These marks can be left on hardwood floors also. The above method works on it as well. A caution here though, not every shoe removes marks.

Many years later I was watching a national TV show, coming from the United States, on handy tips and they showed the same idea. But, when they dragged a white-soled sneaker along the mark, the mark did not disappear. Obviously, the person who prepared the prop for the show was not a handyperson and the guest handyperson did not know that all soles do not remove marks. I found the sole has to be soft rubber, not the hard rubber found on many shoes. I have used, over the years, art erasers, soft-soled shoes, a piece of rubber hose and many other soft, rubbery products, and they worked.

Next time you are in a store, where you will find lots of black marks on the floor, try it. You will be amazed; you might even be offered a job to remove the marks.

The Cure for a Scratchy Piece of Pottery

I'm sure, at one time or another, you have had a piece of pottery, a vase, coffee mug, or ashtray, which is rough on the bottom, you know, the area that is not glazed on which the piece sits during firing. Just pick up any coffee mug; run your finger around on the bottom and you will see what I mean. In most cases, when you slide this mug across a finished table or counter top it will scratch the surface.

You could throw the mug away, but you like the mug, or your favourite aunt Matilda gave it to you. Throwing it away would mean no inheritance! You could try gluing a piece of felt to the bottom. Back in the '50s–before dishwashers–we used to do this with pottery. But, with felt on the bottom, try washing it. How about sandpaper? That would not get it smooth enough. I stumbled onto a simple solution, quite by accident. Once, when I was re-caulking the ceramic tile around the bathtub, I noticed excess caulking, when wiped off the surface, left behind a very thin coating. That observation came in handy one day when my daughter gave me a mug, which scratched my desk.

Obviously, I would not throw the mug away. Sandpaper did not do the job; the surface was still unglazed clay. If I put felt on the bottom, it became impossible to wash, so I put a bead of white, tile-and-tub caulk on the bottom.

I decided the bead of caulking was too thick, so I wiped off the surplus caulking with a wet cloth. This was not quite satisfactory because the surface was a little textured. The final solution: wipe off most of the caulking with a cloth, then dip a cloth into a clear or white liquid dishwashing detergent and wipe the surface smooth, while it is still wet. I turned the mug upside down to let it dry; it worked beautifully. An advantage for boaters, or travelers using an RV: the mugs do not slide.

After my friend, Ron, saw me on TV he went directly to his big boat and caulked all his ashtrays and beer mugs.

"Ron, why not do your dishes too?" I asked him.

"I don't care if my dinner falls overboard but I don't want to lose my beer or my smokes."

Some people's priorities are different.

Extension Cord Dilemma or am I Knots?

"I would like to rearrange the kitchen this summer: the drawers, cupboards and the fridge," my wife informed me.

"Where do you want to start?"

"I'll start with the cutlery drawer and you start over there with that drawer," she answered.

What is there to organize in a cutlery drawer, I ask you. Everything is in a slot and nothing moves… there I go whining again!

She appointed me the organizer of the "junk drawer", my name for it, not hers. She refers to the "junk drawer" as the "drawer we put the things in because we might want to use them again someday before we die" (or not!) drawer. I pulled out a handful of appliance cords and small extension cords.

"What are these?"

"Those are appliance cords," she responded.

I knew that! "Why are we keeping them?"

"Why are we keeping them?" she said. "That one in your right hand is the one from the electric kettle the kids gave us in 1987, and the white one... ." And so it went. I could not throw any of them out on pain of death.

So, here is the knotty problem. The appliance cords that every one of us has stored in a "junk drawer", in the kitchen, will become tangled. They end up as one big ball of endless electrical cord. But, then I'm not telling you anything you do not already know, am I? There are several solutions to this knotty problem. I mean besides just throwing them out, as you will eventually do, after spending far too much time trying to tidy them up.

At one time or another, most of us have tied the cords with small bits of twine, used an elastic or rubber band on them or even used a wire tie. Each of these methods have drawbacks. The string breaks, or you can not get it untied, so you cut it with a knife and maybe yourself at the same time. The elastic, or rubber band, we know can be deadly. It dries out, and the first time you try to remove it, it breaks and snaps you on the knuckles.

"Ouch, that smarts!" I can hear it now.

The wire tie... what can I say about them without using four letter words. The paper pulls off the second time you use it; the wire gets knotted, and you do not know which way to turn it to remove it; or you poke yourself in the end of the finger with the wire and you bleed. Then listen to the shoptalk. In other words there has to be a better way.

A long-time friend, Lynn, uses pipe cleaners as ties. This is a good idea and I have used it many times. Lynn also showed me a way to contain cords, which is nothing short of brilliant. She is an entertainer and carries electronic equipment around, and with this electronic equipment are loose cords. When you have put your big toe through the end of your sock, cut the leg off the foot of the sock and use the leg as a container for cords. Works beautifully. But I digress.

Staring at the mess of cords in the drawer hoping she will take over the job I ask, "I don't know of a way to keep these blasted cords together efficiently. Can you suggest anything?"

"Do the used toilet-paper roll trick," she answered.

You ask, what is the toilet-paper roll trick? You mean you do not know? Well, you have led a sheltered life, have you not? After you have used all the paper from the roll, you are left with a cardboard tube. Aha! The light goes on. Now coil up the toaster cord; you've probably thrown the old toaster out but you still have the cord. Right? You never know when it is going to come in handy, as a leash for the cat, or to tie a mattress on the roof of the car. Stuff the ends of the coiled cord through the tube, the cord will be contained, and neatly. The only thing I have found, with toilet-paper tubes, is they are much like the paper which comes on them: too thin and they will not stand up to rough usage.

I experimented with other cardboard rolls; I even covered the rolls in duct tape to make them stronger, but to no avail. I looked for another method and found I could use a piece of plastic drain pipe, 1 1/4-inch or 1 1/2-inch in size, cut in an appropriate length to suit the cord being stored. The cord stayed in place, the pipe did not break down and everything was neat, tidy and stayed that way.

After using drainpipe to store all of the cords in the drawer I announced: "Okay! I'm finished the drawer. Want to have a look?"

After a lot of fiddly work I'm looking for a little praise here.

"Be right with you," came back to me.

I stood proudly by the drawer, waiting.

"Now that looks better… but…" I heard.

What now, I think. After all that work, am I to be castigated for it?

"That's fine, dear, but those old black tubes look ugly in the drawer. They don't match the decor of the kitchen."

"Since when did anything in the junk drawer have to compliment the kitchen decor?" I asked. "No one will see them, they're inside the drawer."

"Could you do something to make them a little more accept-able?" my wife asked.

Like what? I think. Paint them?

You guys know how foolish a question like that one is. So, I did not ask it.

"I'll try to fix the situation. Make them more presentable," I said.

I spray painted the plastic pipe with decorator colours. Simple!

Since I did not know what each cord was going to be used for, in the future, or from where it came, just by looking at them, I decided to label the tubes with the name of the cords. Remember, you want to know if the cord belongs to the sandwich grill, the one you threw out two years ago because it shorted out and burnt the counter top, or whether it is the cord for the old kettle, which you now use to water the plants. It is a simple matter to label the tubes with the name of the cord by using self-sticking labels. Mark the names of the cords on the labels, and then stick them to the pipe. At this point I would suggest a coat of a clear coat finish, over the label on the pipes, for protection.

I have used this same method for various sized cords in the work-shop as well but I do not paint the tubes. Black plastic goes with anything in the shop.

Since I also have several large extension cords in the shop, to keep sorted out, a similar method is used but with a different type of tube, it works wonders. Visit your favourite flooring store. Ask for one or two of the large, hard cardboard cores from the centre of vinyl yard goods or carpet. Cut the length required to accommodate the extension cord. Mark the length and size of the cord, 25 feet – #12 or what ever, then coil the cord and stuff it into the tube. Put a four inch common nail into a joist overhead, and hang up the coil. There they are, out of the way, but very handy.

Here is one other trick using plastic drainpipe. 1 1/4-inch or 1 1/2-inch pipe can be used effectively to confine the cord on your electric drill, power sander, router and such. Cut a piece of drain pipe to the selected length, drill a hole in one end, run a wire or a piece of tough twine–I use fishing line–through the hole, and fasten to the plug end of the cord. You will not lose it this way. When you are ready to store the tool, just coil up the cord, and stuff it into the plastic drainpipe.

Chapter 7

Squeak, Squawk Get The Chalk

There is no sound in my home, which sets my teeth on edge more than a squeak. It could be a door, a floor, a set of stairs or just about anything you might imagine. I am one who will put jobs off until the-day-after-tomorrow, if I can get away with it, but repairing a squeak takes priority on my to-do list.

Usually a lubricant is required for squeaking wood or plastic. The standard lubricants, which we have in our homes: spray, drippy oils or grease, will not do. They are too messy. Graphite, a black-powdered lubricant, is just too dirty for these jobs. I have found body powder–the sort people use after a bath, to be just what the doctor ordered.

The idea to use powder as a lubricant came to me once when I was powdering the bottom of one of our babies. If you have ever had the dubious honour of doing that you will remember just how slick and smooth the powder makes that little behind. The body powder is dry but slick. You can use it liberally and vacuum up the excess. It will not get sticky and collect dirt as will soap and candle wax. It must, however, be used in dry conditions only. I use unscented body powder. No need to advertise the fact you had a squeaky floor or sticky drawer. If friends or relatives smell the powder you may have to explain and give away your secret.

There is a caution here though. Do not use the powder in anything mechanical. You will gum up the works.

The following handy tips illustrate the use of "body powder" as a lubricant.

Squeaky Hardwood Floors

Squeak... Squeak... Squeak. A sound you do not want to hear when you are trying to sneak in, or at least trying not to wake the kids up as you go downstairs for a second piece of chocolate cake. A squeaky floor is a real nuisance. Can it be fixed? In most cases it can.

Once, when I had this problem in a house, a friend suggested I move; move far away and check the floors in the next house before I bought. Well, this is just a little drastic for such an easily solved problem. You must find what is causing the squeak before you can fix it and that can be the most difficult part of the solution.

The solution, as I said earlier, depends upon the cause. Lets explore the first one and then I will give you my remedy. I hope you are comfortable because this could take some time. If you want to get a hot cup of tea or a cold drink first I do not mind. But, please come back... soon.

One of the causes of squeaks is the hardwood floor itself. Hardwood floors dry out a little and shrink. The pieces now rub on each other as you walk over them. Whether there is a carpet on the floor or not body powder is the answer. I usually keep a large container of an inexpensive, no-name body powder in my workshop. This material is an excellent dry lubricant for wood that rubs or slides on wood. Roll the carpet back if there is one in the room, and sprinkle some powder over the squeaky area. Sweep the powder into the cracks of the floor and sweep up the excess, do not vacuum at this point. If there was a carpet in the room then roll it back down.

If the floor is bare put a scatter rug over the area and tape it to the hardwood floor. If you do not tape it the rug will slide when you step on it and scatter you all over the room. You do not want to bobsled your way to the kitchen do you? If after several days or weeks the squeak has stopped the scatter rug can be removed. Now you can vacuum up the surplus powder.

If you do not vacuum then you will track the powder throughout the house. Over time powder may work its way back to the surface of the floor, from the cracks, as you walk over them. Just keep an eye on the area and vacuum again. A damp tack cloth can pick up excess powder as it does dust on a piece of furniture. (See Chapter 6 the first item, for a description of a tack cloth.)

Dry hardwood flooring is not the only place squeaks can occur. The next story outlines another problem area.

The Tools and Materials Needed are: Body powder, duct tape, broom, tack cloth and vacuum cleaner.

Stopping Squeaks Between Subfloors and Floor Joists

A floor squeak can sometimes be caused by the subfloor rubbing on the floor joist not by the hardwood floor itself. As the house dries and settles, over time, the subfloor shrinks and the floor joists shrink–just a little, enough to cause one to rub on the other and squeak when a person walks on the floor above. The method I am about to describe is simple and usually works. I like to try the simple methods first, and if they work I do not have to go to a lot of effort to solve the problem.

A caution here from a painful experience. One time my wife and I were visiting my brother and his wife. He said, "The floors in the kitchen are squeaking badly. Can't seem to find out why. Could you have a look?"

"Okay. Shouldn't take long. I'll go into the basement and you walk across the floor and I'll mark where they are squeaking."

So, while the women spent a pleasant evening upstairs, my brother and I went to the basement to solve the problem.

I was not as experienced then as I am now. Meaning I had not yet made the many mistakes necessary to give me the experience I have now.

He had some cedar shingles, the type used for shimming when installing trim around windows and doors. I said we could use them to drive between the floor joists and the subfloor. They would stabilize the floor. (It would then have something on which to rest. The floor would not move when walked upon, thus eliminating the squeak.) I had it all worked out, the expert that I was.

We worked all through the evening that I had thought was going to be a relaxing visit, driving shims between subfloor and floor joists.

"How's it going down there?" My sister-in-law hollered down the stairs.

"Just fine. We're finished. Could the two of you walk across the floor for us and see if the squeaks have gone?" I called.

They did the walking and were pleased with the silence.

But, they could see there were waves in the flooring. When we came up from the basement to the kitchen, we could see what looked like the ocean in a storm. Well, not quite, but you get the drift.

What had happened was this. As we drove the shims in-between the subfloor and floor joist we pushed the floor up and the nails, which were not long enough to begin with, poor construction you know, were pushed out of the floor joist and the floor moved up. Soooooooo, back to the dungeon and pull all the shims out. Now we had to find away to get the floor down to the floor joist and flat. I will describe how we did that in the next story, but first a simpler method of solving this problem.

The Tools and Materials Needed are: Body powder and a plastic–squeeze bottle, with a pointed spout. (The type of bottle in which you find mustard or ketchup.) Fill the bottle right to the top with body powder and put the lid back on tightly. Put the spout of the bottle into the space between the floor joist and the subfloor and squeeze. The powder blows into the space and settles onto the top of the floor joist. Now, when the subfloor rubs on the floor joist it will slide silently instead of squeaking. Problem solved.

Please use all safety precautions: solid stepladder, bright light, safety goggles and a face mask over your mouth and nose. You do not want powder blowing back into your eyes and you do not want it in your lungs.

Squeak of Nail Through Subfloor Into Floor Joist

The successful method my brother and I used for his squeaky floor follows. A lot of work but it was worth the effort in his case.

As I said, sometimes the squeak in a floor is caused by the shrinkage, through drying, of the floor joist or the subfloor. As the floor joists and the subfloor dry and shrink, they pull apart just a little. As a person walks across the floor it moves up and down. The nail holding the subfloor in place now begins to move up and down in its the hole in the floor joist and the squeak begins. Or, the subfloor rubs on the top of the floor joist and the squeak begins. One way to correct this is to fasten a support to the floor joist and to the subfloor, a piece of angle iron will do the trick, thus supporting the subfloor and stopping the movement.

Pre-drill the angle iron, on both flanges, at centers of about one foot with a bit specifically meant to drill through steel. The size bit will be determined by the size of screw you have selected for use. Place the angle iron against the floor joist and tightly against the subfloor. Screw the angle iron first to the floor joist with 1 1/4-inch screws, then to the subfloor with the 3/4-inch screws. This should support the subfloor and stop the movement of the floor. In my brother's case we positioned the angle irons just below the subfloor and when we put the screws into the subfloor they pulled the floor down to the angle iron thus eliminating the squeak and the ripple effect.

I would suggest a little body powder on the top of the angle iron, just as a precaution against a squeak developing here. Instead of body powder on the angle iron you could use construction adhesive. It welds the whole package together, so to speak.

The Tools and Materials Needed are: Coarse threaded-screws #10 or #12–1 1/4–inch and 3/4–inch in length (this length will depend upon the thickness of the subfloor), an electric drill, screwdriver, ladder, safety glasses, mask and several pieces of angle iron, in lengths easily handled. Angle iron can be purchased at a hardware store or building centre.

Supporting Squeaky Subfloor at Floor Joints

Sometimes the squeak in a floor is caused by the nonsupport of a joint between the plywood sheets. Where two sheets join in the space between the floor joists the sheets could flex and rub against one another. In today's houses this should not happen as most contractors use tongue and groove plywood or chipboard as a subfloor. Many contractors also use construction adhesive on all joints and on the top of the floor joists before installation. This makes the subfloor and floor joists one.

If your floor squeak is caused by movement between the sheets of subfloor or shrinking at the tongue and groove joint you can fix it using the following method.

Cut pieces of 2 X 4 to fit tightly between the floor joists at the joint in the subfloor. Before nailing the pieces to the joists put a bead of construction adhesive on the top of the 2 X 4 next to the subfloor. Then toenail in place tightly against the floor at the joint. The construction adhesive will weld the 2 X 4 to the subfloor and they will become one eliminating the squeak.

The Tools and Materials Needed are: A hammer, saw, ladder, some 2 1/2-inch nails, and construction adhesive some pieces of 2 X 4. Please use all safety precautions: solid stepladder, bright light, safety goggles, a face mask over your mouth and nose and protective gloves.

Squeaky Stairs: another Annoyance

Squeaky stairs announce someone approaching. It can be an advantage to have at least one tread squeak on the stairs. This will let you or your dog know someone is coming up or down the stairs. If you are alone in the house you can think about whether it is a ghost or a burglar. Either way you want to know about it.

Whether it is a squeak or a squawk the fixing of it is not as easy as the other squeaks and squawks to repair.

Investigate by going under the stairs and listening as someone else walks on the offending tread or treads. Listen for the location of the squeak. It will be in one or more of the following places: between tread and riser, between tread and stringer or between riser and stringer.

If you have a well-made set of stairs you will likely find small blocks were glued to the underside of the riser and the tread where it joins the tread. This makes the two components as one. If this is where the squeak is on your stairs, then make some small blocks, about 1 1/4-inches X 1 1/4-inches and about 4-inches long. Have someone heavy stand on that tread and then glue and screw the blocks to the riser and the tread. If the squawk is between the tread and stringer do the same thing and your problem should stop. Now you can sneak down stairs to the fridge for a piece of that forbidden pie, undetected, before you go to sleep. Ain't life grand?

The Tools and Materials Needed are: Several pieces of birch or maple 1 1/4-inches X 1 1/4-inches X 4-inches, carpenters glue, 1 5/8-inch flat head wood-screws and an electric drill and drill bits.

Squeaking Hinges a Natural Burglar Alarm?

The unnerving sound of the kitchen door opening can send shivers up your spine. It also announces to the other member of the family that you are about to cheat on your diet.

"I'm going to fix the squeak in that kitchen door before it drives me around the bend." I said to my wife one Saturday.

"No, that's not necessary it doesn't sound bad at all. I hardly even notice it," she said it with a smile on her face.

You know the look. The one which says I am being sly and you do not know why. It was not until several years later I learned she stopped me from fixing the squeak because it acted as an alarm for her, told her of my comings and goings.

To solve the problem of the squeaky door you must understand the cause. As I said, a squeaky hinge can work to ones advantage sometimes by acting as an announcement someone has come into the room or the house. But, what if it is you who wants to come or go without the movement being announced? So I guess the only thing to do is fix it. Is this a simple trick? Not always. Sometimes it is only one hinge squeaking.

Have one person open and close the door slowly while you put your ear next to one of the hinges, do not get it caught in the door, that could smart. If that hinge does not squeak then you know it is the other one. However, I suggest you work on both hinges because if only one is squeaking now, the other will soon.

Today most, if not all, door hinges are made of steel. Bare steel rusts. Rust makes a hinge squeak. The pin has rusted or the sleeve enclosing the pin has rust on the inside or both. Most often we pull the pin, and oil it and put the oil into the pin sleeve. This works for a short time but it is just a band-aid. The squeak will likely start again in a few weeks.

The permanent solution is as simple to perform as the above band-aid solution. Remove the pin from the hinge plates. Clean off the rust. I use medium steel wool and penetrating oil. Penetrating oil is made to penetrate into the rust. A light machine oil can be used but it is not as effective. Put the oil on the steel wool and clean the pin until it shines. Next roll the steel wool into a rope or snake between your hands. Run the oily rope up and down in the sleeves of the hinge plates. This will clean the rust out.

Now, run a small cloth through the same sleeve to remove the bits and pieces of steel wool, they rust faster than the hinge does. Before returning the pin to the hinge oil it well with light machine oil and the rust will not likely return for a long time.

Preventative maintenance is advisable though. Oil the pin at least once a year. Now you can sneak in and out without detection. I think you will find the hinges, which squeak most often, are on doors to rooms with a lot of humidity, garages, bathrooms and kitchens.

The Tools and Materials Needed are: Screwdriver, hammer, medium steel wool, gloves, penetrating oil, light machine oil, and a cotton cloth.

Not the Hinge Squeaking?

In this case the squeak could mean that the door is rubbing on the doorstop. The doorstop is the 1 5/8-inch piece of trim on the face of the doorjamb. This is the piece of trim which keeps the door from swinging right on through into the other room. As the trim, doors and house dry over the years the doors sometimes rub on the doorstop. To fix this problem use a hammer and a piece of 1 X 2 wood, about 12-inches long. Pine, spruce or hardwood will do nicely. Put one edge of the piece of 1 X 2 against the doorstop and lightly tap it with a hammer. The doorstop will move ever so slightly and the door will no longer rub on it when it is closed or opened.

The Tools and Materials Needed are: A hammer, piece of 1 X 2 wood about 12-inches long.

Chapter 8

Little Things Mean a Lot

I pride myself on being a thoughtful person. My wife agrees with me. She will also tell you I spend a lot of time being thoughtful. I think about all the ways I can get out of doing the home repair, maintenance and decorating jobs, around the house.

In life it is the little things which seem to mean so much: that special birthday card, an anniversary card, or flowers for no reason at all. It is not just the romantic, "little things" which mean so much, but the little home repairs being completed, mean a lot; such things as the drafty front door, dripping faucet in the bathroom or even the sticky lock on the back door. Not only will they make that special someone in your life feel happier, but, who knows you might even save some money and energy, as well. This chapter is about, "the little things".

Lubricating Locks... One Puff Will Do!

Lubricating a door lock is a simple matter. Just put the spout of the oilcan into the key way and squirt, right? How tough can that be? This is what most people would do.

When I was in the lumber business I learned something, from a lock manufacturer, about oil and locks. Oil could be the lock's worst enemy this applies to all locks: house, car, cabinet or padlock. It was explained to me, that liquid lubricants can attract dust and could eventually, "gum up the works", so to speak. So, what to use? Something dry and slick will do the trick. In Chapter 7, I suggested using body powder on floors to stop squeaking... I said it was dry and slick. **Do not use it for locks.** It absorbs moisture in locks. So what should one use?

I was told to use powdered graphite in all locks. You can buy powdered graphite in any hardware store and most lumberyards. It usually comes in a small soft tube with a pointed spout and a threaded top. Remove the top. Place the spout in the lock and squeeze. Squeeze, very, verrrrry, gently to puff the powder into the lock cylinder. Squeeze hard and it will blow back and get you. To avoid getting the powdered graphite back on your hands, and your clothes, when you squeeze too energetically, place a paper towel over the cylinder. Try puncturing a small hole in the paper first and put the spout of the tube through it. The paper will catch any blow-back which might occur. Only a little graphite is required to lubricate a lock; it goes a long way. This product is really dirty, but it works.

After using the powdered graphite, you will find, when putting the key in the lock the first few times, it will come out a little black. Just wipe it off with a tissue. Soon, no more black will come out of the cylinder.

One evening, I lubricated the lock on the front door of the office in which I worked with several others. The boss came to work the next morning, with his hands full. He juggled his load while fumbling for his key, unlocked the door, and stuck the key in his mouth until he was able to set his load down. When the rest of us came to work that morning we got a real shock and thought the boss was having a heart attack or something. His lips were black. We asked him if he was all right and received an affirmative answer. We pointed out that his lips were black, he went to look and washed it off. Then, the investigation began into what had caused this. Soon, I realized the graphite had done the trick and told everyone about it. We all had a good laugh but we also learned a lesson.

To Weather Strip or not to Weather Strip, That is the Question.

Little cracks do not crack me up, they simply mean work. At one time I was a partner in an air sealing company: we tested homes for air leaks. We used what was, for those days, a very sophisticated system.

After removing the front door we put a large fan in the opening, and sucked the air out of the house. Before the fan was turned on, all openings such as fireplaces, range hoods and vents were blocked. The fan was turned on, and the technicians worked around the interior of the home, with smoke markers, to find air leaks, as the fan sucked the air out. I was amazed to discover air leaks in unexpected areas. I, of course, expected leaks at doors and windows, but along baseboards or around interior doors? Wow! That was something else! Houses built in the last few years are being better sealed, as they are built. No costly after market sealing, today.

A computer was used to measure the amount of air exiting the house. We found if we added together all of the air leaks from cracks and holes they would be equal to a hole in the wall about 3-feet X 3-feet. You would certainly fix that hole so why not fix the small ones?

The more obvious leaks are around doors and windows. Even the smallest crack around a door loses as much air as a visibly larger hole. For example: a 1/4-inch crack under an exterior door may not look like much of a space to you but, if the door is 36-inches wide, that crack lets as much cold air in, and hot air out, as a hole through the door 3-inch x 3-inch. Do the calculations: 36-inches x 1/4-inch = 9-square inches, a hole 3-inch x 3-inch. If you had a hole that big in your door, I will bet you would fix it! Doing the same type of calculation for a 1/4-inch crack all around your present door represents… a hole 6-inch x 10-inch. Little cracks do mean a lot. As I understand it, the seen and unseen cracks and crevices in your exterior walls, and around windows and doors, could account for some 33% of the heat lost from your home.

If you want to find those "energy robbers" you can do this: on a windy day, look at the curtains on the windows. If they are blowing but the windows are not open, you have found substantial air leakage, which needs your attention first.

If you want to find other guilty windows and doors, try another trick. On a windy day tape a piece of tissue paper, a strip about 1 1/2-inch wide and 4-inches long, to a coat hanger, hold it near the edges of the windows and doors. When the paper waves in the breeze you know you have found an "energy robber". Now that you have found the crevices, seal them by using paintable caulking. Then weather-strip around doors and windows. You can cut your heating bill down considerably.

As you have noticed through out this book, I like to put a little humour in my stories, but there is nothing humorous about "energy robbers".

Raising a Stink About Unwanted Odors

Sometimes we are faced with locating and eliminating a nasty odor in a closet, under a sink or in some confined area. There are several things which can be done to rid the area of an unpleasant smell. First you have to find what is causing the smell. Follow your nose, on this one. Sniff out the odor; you may find some piece of food, liquid or old sock is the culprit.

One time we had a nasty odor coming from the basement in the laundry room. It got worse as the days went on. We finally traced it to the area where the food freezer sat. We sniffed around and around the area, until the little stinker was found.

One of us had set a package of frozen hamburger on the table beside the freezer, and it had slipped off the table and down behind the freezer. After thawing out it started to rot. By the time we got to it the stench was pretty strong. Getting rid of the smell of rotten meat is a tough job. We sprayed, and powdered and aired, but it still hung heavy in the air.

No matter where the odor is coming from you must find the cause, then eliminate it. It could be that package of hamburger, or it could be something under the kitchen sink. If it is under the sink you must take everything out of the cabinet. But be prepared, it can be a disgusting sight: old, rusty pieces of steel scouring pads, empty cleanser cans, with rusted metal rims, empty old, liquid, dishwashing detergent bottles and other things you may not be able to identify. If, like us, you keep the day's garbage in a container under there, as well as the empty pop containers and assorted bottles for recycling, you might find these are causing the odor. Most likely it is a piece of apple or potato peel that missed the garbage container last Sunday, and has started to decompose. Not a pretty sight.

After cleaning out the cupboard, you could spray with a nice-smelling deodorant. But there is a better way, less expensive and environmentally friendly. A listener to my radio show told me this method one Saturday morning. She identified herself as "getting on in years" and told me what her grandmother used to do to get rid of odors. She would pour about an inch of "white or clear" vinegar into a small bowl. Her grandmother then put the bowl into the cupboard in a corner or wherever the "stink" was found, and left it there until the odor was gone. And it will go, trust me. I have a bowl under the kitchen sink and it keeps the cabinet smelling fresh. This is a very inexpensive method and, as I have said, environmentally friendly.

This Tip Could Make You Cry-It is So Simple

After you read this tip you will wonder if I am crazy or have worked at this book too long. If the truth were known: it is probably a little bit of both.

I have never tried this trick for removing the odor of paint from a room but I have had several people swear that it works. Next time you paint, and the room is heavy with paint odor, give it a try.

Put some cold water in a bowl; the larger the room the larger the bowl, or the more bowls you must use. Cut a cooking onion in large chunks, and toss the chunks into the water. Set the bowl in the stinky room and shut the doors. Let it stand over night, and then check it out. My listeners told me that the room would smell sweet again. I wonder if you can use the onions after that? Only kidding.

Fill Cracks in Plaster and Keep the Filler in Place

This is one of those tricks I learned from experience. Early in our marriage, we lived in an old house, and when I say old I mean very old. How old was it? It was so old the plaster had horsehair as a binder in the brown coat, the undercoat, which is put on before the white finish. The lath under the plaster was wooden strips, about 3/8-inch thick X 1 5/8-inch wide, nailed horizontally to the studs with spaces between so the brown or scratch coat, as it was sometimes called, would key between and bond. As the old houses dried, and the lath shrank, the plaster cracked.

We wanted to paint the walls, get rid of the look of the faded, old, flowered wallpaper. To do it right, we had to take off the old wallpaper–an easy job, in this case, because there were so many layers, and they were so dried out, they almost fell off by themselves. I say almost because I did have to wet them down and peel the layers off. But that is another story.

"Just paint over the paper," my mother-in-law said.

I knew better. Painting over layer upon layer of paper just does not work. (See Chapter 3, page 22, for how to do this, if you must.)

After removing the paper I found the plaster surface looked like a road map of Toronto–cracks everywhere. The larger ones had to be filled. I scraped the loose plaster out of the cracks and put in crack filler. Next it I sanded the filler and painted, starting with a primer of course. After a year or so the filler started to fall out. I wondered why. This was one of those times I let the problem whirl around in my brain for a while and the solution soon began to appear.

The reason the filler fell out of the cracks was because it did not properly bond to the old, very dry, plaster. I decided if I wet the crack with clean water the wet filler would bond more easily. In other words, the water in the filler would not be absorbed into the old plaster causing the filler to dry out, then fall out. I tried this method and it worked. I have been recommending the procedure ever since.

So, here is the drill. Use an old screwdriver–I keep one around for just such jobs–and clean out the crack. With the crevice tool, on your vacuum cleaner take out all the old, loose plaster and dust. Next, use a clean paintbrush and brush clean, cool water into the crack, then apply the filler. Smooth with a putty knife and you are done. The time taken with surface preparation will show in your finished job.

Just as an aside, I have a friend whose company packages concrete crack-filler. When I told him about this method, he said he was going to put it into the instructions for his concrete patch material.

The Tools and materials required are: An old screwdriver, vacuum cleaner with crevice tool, clean paint brush, clean container of cool water and a good quality crack filler meant for plaster.

Putting a Nail in a Plaster Wall

Here is another one of those pesky little jobs, which, when done properly, will earn you lots of brownie points. The job is hanging a picture of Great-Aunt Gertrude or grumpy, old Uncle Joshua. You have been putting it off because you just hate trying to put a nail in plaster. It cracks, spalls (flakes) or just will not take the nail without a lot of mess. Here is "Hammarman" to the rescue. If you were putting the nail in wood panelling or planking or even drywall you could just pound the nail in, but in plaster it is a whole different thing. Putting one nail in plaster is troublesome, but to hang a picture properly and straight, takes two nails–double trouble. (Read Chapter 6, Dust Catcher, page 22)

When it comes to putting a nail in plaster I find there is only one way to do it. Drill a hole first. But, how do you drill a hole which will take a nail, and not be a loose fit? Easy, use a nail for a drill bit. Yes, that is right, use a nail for a drill bit. Use a spiral finishing nail, the same size as the one on which you will hang the picture; they make good one-time drill bits. With a pair of sidecutters cut the head off a nail, the size you are about to use. Put it in the electric drill. Stick a piece of masking tape over the spot you want to drill, it helps keep the plaster from spalling, and drill. The job will be done and the nail you use will fit snugly into the hole. Drill again for the second nail, hang the picture and collect those brownie points.

The Tools and materials required are: A small nail hammer, pencil, 1 1/2-inch spiral finish nails, measuring tape, level, side cutters, masking tape, electric drill and a paper or foam cup

Cleaning Ceramic Tile Grout or Getting Rid of Grunge

Does the ceramic tile in your shower stall or bathtub surround look bright and shiny new or…? Probably "or", if you are like most people. What makes a tile wall look grungy is likely the dirty, graying grout. If you wipe the tile down after each shower, (I use a squeegee, like the ones used for windows, to wipe down my tile.) the tile will look great, but the grout can get gray with time and use. Old grout gets gray and grungy looking, because it absorbs soap and water. Today, a nonabsorbent, or almost non-absorbent grout can be purchased. Since it does not absorb the soapy water it should not turn gray as readily as the old grouting materials.

Cleaning grout is simple. There are many commercial grout cleaners. If you purchase one of these remember: after you clean the grout it must be sealed. When sealed the grout is not as likely to become grey again for quite some time. Read the instructions on the container because you may get a surprise. I bought a cleaner for our tile walls and found **"Do not use on fibreglass, vinyl and other synthetic materials"**. Our shower wall was ceramic tile, but the shower floor was made of fibreglass. We could not use the cleaner we bought. I suggest before buying any cleaner, check the material your tub or shower floor is made of.

I said this chapter was about the little things, but I did not say doing the little things was easy or took little time. Cleaning the grout is one job which does take some time, but it is worth the effort.

A Different Way to Hold a Gluejoint!

Here is a neat little trick I learned from my Grandpa Mac, many, many years ago. It is simple but it works every time.

When you need a weight to hold a gluejoint in place it is handy to have something that is heavy, clean and preferably soft as well. A brick does quite well. You might say a brick is not usually clean and you'd be right. You might also say a brick is rough and would mark the work. Right again! You would also say a brick is not soft and you are right there, too. Boy, you catch on fast! You could say those are the hard facts. (Pun intended.) However, all of these things can be easily overcome. Wrapping the brick in several layers of brown paper, such as that used in grocery bags, will prevent it from scratching or soiling the work. The "brick-trick" is good only if the weight is required on a flat, even surface.

If you need to put weight on an uneven surface, a brick will not do. I keep a small bag of ordinary sand in my workshop, for just such occasions. Put as much sand in a plastic sandwich bag as you require. This weighted bag will mould itself around the material to be glued and the weight will be evenly distributed.

If the project to be glued is an uneven shape on top and bottom, it will be difficult to set it flat on the workbench. Again, use bagged sand but this time use two, lay one on the workbench and put the uneven project on it. The project will nestle down into the sand, and you are ready to glue and weight it with the other. Pretty ingenious, eh? Thanks Grandpa Mac.

Is It Latex Or Oil Base Paint?

When repainting, it is necessary to determine whether the surface is presently painted with oil based paint or latex paint. Without special treatment, you will have difficulty keeping latex paint on a surface previously painted with oil based paint.

If you are in a quandary as to whether the paint on your wall is latex or oil base, there is a simple test to determine which it is. Soak a cotton ball with rubbing alcohol and rub the cotton ball on the wall. If the paint comes off on the cotton ball it is latex. If the paint does not come off then it is oil base. Remember though, that some paints oxidize. This means your paint may have a chalky surface to it and that may be what you took off with the alcohol. Rub the same spot with a clean cotton ball soaked in alcohol. If the paint comes off again it is latex. Do this in an inconspicuous place. Only do this in an obvious place if you are going ahead with the painting; the mark on the wall will be unsightly. Since you now know which type of paint is on the wall, you can give the surface the treatment and primer it requires. Wow, is that simple or what?

Chapter 9

Fasteners-Some History

In this chapter we will nail down some hard facts about things like screws, bolts and nails.

Nails

"Nail" is a word with which we are all familiar, and which we use from time to time, but what does it mean? I looked it up in several dictionaries and was amazed at the number of definitions. The one we would most likely hear, in this book, refers to a product used for fastening together pieces of wood.

Simply put, a nail is a slender piece of metal having a point and a head, and is used for driving into wood or through wood, etc., as for fastening pieces together.

This is a simple definition for a complicated group of products.

Which is the correct type of nail to use for the project? What length of nail should you use? Are there nails meant for use indoors and nails meant for use outdoors? The answer to the last is yes.

In most plans and patterns printed in the United States the size of a nail is referred to in "penny" sizes. Originally, the "penny" designation referred to the cost, in pennies, of nails per hundred, but now better describes the size. In plans and patterns from the U.S.A. the short form for penny is "d", such as "4d". Sizes start with 2d, which is an inch. The following chart lists the approximate lengths, which are represented as "penny" size, for convenient translation into Canadian sizes. Please, keep in mind this table is for comparison only and cannot be considered exact.

Approximate Size Comparison of Penny Designation and Length

Penny Size	2d	3d	4d	5d	6d	7d	8d	9d	10d	12d	16d	20d
Approx. Size	1"	1 1/4"	1 1/2"	1 3/4"	2"	2 1/4"	2 1/2"	2 3/4"	3"	3 1/4"	3 1/2"	4"

Nails are made of different types of metal: steel, aluminum, or copper. Some of the most commonly used nails are listed below, but specialty nails can be purchased for projects that will not use a common type of nail. Nails are made for specific types of fastening. Always choose the correct type of nail for your job.

Drywall nails are made for the installation of plasterboard or drywall. The most common of these nails are **ringed** for a better hold. The head is quite broad and the point is extremely sharp. Watch out when you reach into your nail pouch, you can stab yourself–I have–and it hurts.

Common nails are for rough construction purposes: for nailing heavy lumber together, as in framing a house. Today's common nails are now spiraled or twisted, for greater holding power, and therefore, you can use a shorter nail than if you used a straight nail; check manufacturer's specifications.

Finishing nails suit finer work, as the name implies, like trimming and cabinetry. You can buy finishing nails in aluminum and stainless steel for special projects. They come spiraled as well as straight. The smaller finishing nails 1–inch and shorter, are not twisted.

Roofing Nails are usually made of galvanized material, so they will not rust, and are used with ashphalt shingles. Aluminum roofing nails can be usd on asphalt roofing but are a must for aluminum roofing. They are slightly higher in price.

Underlay nails are usually a blue colour, are used to fasten sheets of plywood or composite underlay sheets, to the subfloor before a finished floor like tile or sheet goods is installed. These nails are ringed to make them stay put, and, believe me they do stay put. (See chapter 5, page 50, "We'll Just Spend A Few Bucks", for my experience with these nails.)

The above are only a few of the more common nails found at your favourite lumber or hardware store. Always use the proper nail for the job. Do not make do with a nail just because you happen to have it. Buy the **correct** nail and you will be rewarded with a solid job.

Screws

Anyone who has had to assemble a piece of furniture, children's toys, or any knock–down type of project, or has made a project from scratch, knows there is more than one type of screw or bolt head. In the beginning, there was a slot head screw. This was the easiest type of screw for our forefathers to make. Once they mastered the making of the threaded piece of metal, it was a simple matter to cut a slot in the flat head, of the screw or bolt. A flat-blade screwdriver must be used with the slotted screw or bolt. Under torque, a flat-bladed driver has a tendency to slip out of the slot. Often, damage occurs to the surface of the project and even to your knuckles. Later, two types of screw-heads were developed to take the slip out of the turning of a screw or bolt.

In the U.S.A.–the Philips head was developed. This is a double slotted head: each slot runs at right angles to the other. There are different sized slots, for different sized heads.

In Canada, a different head was developed: the Robertson head, which has a square hole in the head in place of slots. There are several sizes of Robertson heads as well.

The larger screw head, required a larger square hole in the head. Robertson screwdrivers have colour-coded handles, to make it easy to determine which size you will require.

They start with black: this is the largest screwdriver and the sizes go down from there, red, green and yellow. Yellow is the smallest of the common sizes. There are other sizes but these are the most used sizes. Incidentally the most commonly used screwdriver is red.

The automotive industry, it seems, began using a different type of head all together, the Torx head. Simply described, it is a variation of the Phillips head with three slots running at angles to each other. It takes a special type of driver to operate the Torx head and these come in different size heads as well.

Although Roberston and Phillips head screws are the most commonly used screws in the construction industry, the Torx head screw was recently introduced in some areas of construction. Because the driver is less likely to slip out of this type of head than other types. The Torx head screw can now be found in use for decking, railings, stair treads and more.

Chapter 10

The Toolbox

Tools are just an extension of our mind and body. I have heard that tools were around before verbal communication. They were strong, heavy and sharp objects for pounding, scraping and cutting. Today tools can mean anything from simple hammers to complicated electronics. Over the centuries human beings have used tools to supplement their strength, ability to separate and, now to compute and save data. This book was written on a computer. The computer has become the tool of my trade now; I have exchanged my carpenter's tools for a computer.

My Grandpa Mac always said, "A poor tradesman blames a poor job on his tools. But, even a good tradesman will have a difficult time doing a good job with poor tools. Good tools, and the proper tools for the job, do make a difference."

In order to assemble the Toolbox I talked to many people, and read many books on tools. I found no one has a perfect answer for the perfect toolbox. Your choice of tools will depend upon your needs, based on the type of work you might be required to do, or the size of your living accommodations and storage space available. With all this in mind, I suggest the following tool list for a standard handyperson toolbox. The contents of your toolbox will probably vary somewhat from this list.

When you select your tools, buy the best quality you can afford. If you do not have the money to buy the best, when will you have the money to replace the inferior tools you bought?

My thanks to Stanley Tools of Canada for helping me with the information for these pages, and for the knowledge about tools their staff have shared with me over the years.

Tools for the Job

My grandfather said it to me first, then many decades later my son said it to me, before we started an addition to our house, "There's a proper tool for every job and that's the tool you must use."

I have, over the years, found this to be worth remembering and applying to every job I do. A great many do-it-yourselfers, make do, with improper tools. A prime example of this is the screwdriver. It is probably the most misused tool in the box. It is used as a paint stirrer, pry bar, chisel, scraper, and, oh, yes, sometimes even as a screwdriver. In that case it is sometimes used even though it is not the correct driver for the screw. Making do with it, even though it is too small or too big or the wrong type is a mistake.

For the everyday jobs around the house, I have two portable toolboxes. The first is red, for emergencies in plumbing and wiring. In this box I have all the tools and bits and pieces, like twist connectors, electrical tape, solder, copper caps and elbows. With all of these, plus the correct pliers, screwdrivers, wire cutter, pipe cutter, hammer, hacksaw and torch, I can tackle almost any electrical or plumbing emergency, and you will be able to as well.

My second toolbox, which is blue, holds carpentry tools, for any woodworking problem. If I need to hang a picture, fix a squeaky door or floor I have the tools. This box has a hammer; full set of screwdrivers; 1/2-inch wood chisel; a 16-foot measuring tape; small, lighted, magnetic level; SharpTooth saw, for cutting wood; wire cutter; several sizes of pliers; a try square; Wonderbar and a tool, that is commonly called a "cheese-grater plane"–a Surform plane. My son, Jim, taught me the trick of using two different boxes for home repairs and I have found it extremely efficient.

When someone borrows a tool from either toolbox, it is generally not put back; just laid on the workbench. If the borrower does remember to put it back, it is likely to be put back in the wrong box, which messes up the organization. To solve this problem I put a dab of red paint on the tools for the red box. On the tools for the blue box I put a dab of–what else–blue paint. This does not guarantee that it will be put back into the correct box, but at least I will know where it does belong when I see it.

If I can not find the tool I am looking for anywhere in the house, then I assume Jim has borrowed it. Right now Jim has my entire blue carpenter's box at his house… I do not know if I will see it back, unless I go fetch it myself.

Some of the specialty tools in the blue box should be explained. The Surform plane has been on the market since at least 1960, when I built my first house. If you look at one in the store, you will see it looks like a hand plane, but instead of a single blade, it has a series of small sharp cutters. The blades look very much like those of a cheese-grater. Hence, many people refer to it as, that "cheese-grater" tool. With the Surform, even an inexperienced handyperson can plane the end of a piece of wood. The end grain is the most difficult part of a piece of wood to smooth, with a hand plane. The Surform is also a very good tool for shaping plasterboard.

I mentioned a SharpTooth saw. Most handy people find cutting a piece of wood, by hand, is very tedious. With the SharpTooth you can crosscut a piece of wood almost as easily as you can cut a piece of bread. The teeth on this type of saw are twelve teeth to the inch and very aggressive. One tooth cuts on the down stroke, one tooth on the up stroke, and a third tooth cleans the sawdust out of the cut, making the going much easier.

There are at least two sizes of SharpTooth saws. One is standard 24-inches, used in the workshop, and the other, being 15-inches, fits nicely into your portable toolbox. If you look at the handle, on the latter, you will find the leading edge of the handle forms a right angle with the back of the saw blade, and the under side of the handle forms a 45-degree angle with the back of the saw blade. So, you can eliminate the try square and combination square from your toolbox, for those angle-cuts.

Most people feel that a measuring tape, is a measuring tape, is a measuring tape–but not so. Here are some features to look for in a good tape. Look for a triple riveted hook, on the end of the pull-out blade. Triple rivets help prevent the hook from breaking loose from the blade. A 1-inch or 3/4-inch wide blade is most useful. Blades of these widths will remain rigid, allowing you to measure to the top of a wall, without the tape bending before you can reach the top. They are also strong enough to slide across the floor for many feet to another wall so you will not need help from a second person.

An intriguing tape is one called the "top-read tape". If you have ever had to measure the space between two walls, for example, you know that it is easy to make a mistake in the measurement. With a regular tape, you must read the measurement on the tape, and add on the length of the tape case, 2 1/4-inches or 3 1/2-inches or whatever yours is, to get the proper measurement. When adding measurements, which include fractions, we often add incorrectly then cut the piece of wood too long or too short. The top-read tape eliminates these mistakes. The top of the tape case has a window in it, with a red line showing the exact spot of the correct measurement. This tape is not available in all stores, and you may have to look for some time before you find one. It is definitely worth the look.

I have seen new measuring devises on the market. They use infrared light to measure from one wall to another. Excellent for one-person operations, and I understand they are quite accurate.

Grandpa Mac gave me a piece of advice relating to measurement. It may seem obvious, but think about it: "No matter how often you cut a piece of wood it never gets any longer. So measure twice and cut once."

Hammar's Suggestions for Tools to Buy and Why

Hammers: You will find in a book on tools many types of hammers, but the type you will most likely need is the claw hammer. I think we have all used a claw hammer with a wooden handle, at sometime. If you have ever broken one of these handles, you know how difficult it is to replace it. I use a fibreglass-handled hammer. The handle absorbs the shock of striking and gives strength for pulling nails. If you are going to do much building or heavy hammering, then using a 16-ounce hammer would be best. It will be heavy enough for construction, and light enough for other work, after you have finished the construction.

There are many different types of shanks, (handles) for hammers: resin, fibreglass and graphite, to name a few, so choose the one you like best. It has been said that some solid steel handles do not absorb shock, so it can be hard on your arm if you use it for a long period of time.

Mallets: You will be required to strike a piece of wood in many projects, and not leave a mark. This is difficult to do with a steel-headed hammer. A rubber-headed mallet, preferably white rubber, is the tool required.

Wonderbar: When we need to pull a nail, we often resort to the claw hammer. It is suitable for small nails but larger ones will require a pry bar of some type. This is why I suggest the Wonderbar for the toolbox. Its thin, flat surface makes it easy to get under nailheads and to pry them out. It also works well if you must pry apart two pieces of wood. And you will find it fits easily into any toolbox.

Measuring Tapes: The most desirable tape measure is made of steel, with a hook fastened to its 3/4-inch or 1-inch blade, with at least, three rivets. A case with a soft rubber pad to cushion the return of the tape will save wear and tear on the hook at the end of the tape. A wide tape blade makes measuring vertically and horizontally much easier. I prefer the top-read tape myself. There are also electronic tapes, which measure with infrared and give you a read out in a window in the top of the tape.

Try Square: This is a right-angle tool, with a steel or aluminum blade, usually 8-inches in length, and a wooden or plastic handle. It is used to mark right-angles, for assembly or cutting. You do not need a try square or combination square if you are using, a SharpTooth saw. (See saws, above.)

Combination Square: This type of square is more useful than the try square as you can mark 90-degree and 45-degree angles. The head will slide along the blade making it easier to mark the different angles.

Rafter Squares: This right-angle square has a 16-inch blade and a 24-inch blade. If you learn to use the rafter square you will find it one of the most helpful tools in your collection.

Spring Clamps: Spring clamps are handy for holding pieces while you cut, paint or glue. They come in several sizes. Two sizes, a pair of 6-inch and a pair of 9-inch, would be ideal for your toolbox.

Screwdrivers: There are four types of screwdrivers, which you will require. Select the screwdriver best suited to your needs.
   Flat tip: This will be used for slotted screws. Avoid these screws if possible, they are not easy to install.
   Phillips: This type is used for screws which have a "+" shaped slot. Phillips screws should be removed and installed with the proper screwdriver tip. You will find this type of screw used mostly in products assembled in the U.S.A.
   Robertson: The Robertson screw and driver are, I have been told, a Canadian invention, and will not likely be found in the U.S.A. I

have found this type of screw is more easily installed and removed, with less slippage, than other common types of screws.

Torx: This screwdriver and screw/bolt was introduced, as I understand it, by the automotive industry. They felt they could put more torque on a screw or bolt of this type of head, without it slipping, than conventional screws or bolts. It has been described as a better type of screw and has found its way into the construction industry.

Handsaws: A variety of saws can be stored in your toolbox but you need to decide which you will use most, and then buy those. Some of the most common are outlined below.

SharpTooth: This saw comes in two sizes, 15-inch for the toolbox, and 24-inch for the shop. Since I use a power saw in the shop, I find the only handsaw I use is the 15-inch, SharpTooth. This saw has a handle, which, forms a right angle or a 45-degree angle with the back of the blade, and so can act as a try square or combination square, (see try square and combination square above) and the teeth are very aggressive. There are three different types of teeth: one cuts on the down stroke, one cuts on the up stroke and the other clears the saw-kerf. (The cut)

Hacksaw: The hacksaw is meant to cut metal; it has a small-toothed, close-set blade. This saw will cut through steel, aluminum, and copper. It will also, because of its teeth, cut plastic and even china. Once I had to cut a toilet bowl, for a prop at a home show; I used a hacksaw and it worked

Drywall Saw: This is a short-bladed, sharp-pointed saw, with coarse teeth, meant to cut drywall. When you need to cut a hole in the middle of a sheet, force the pointed blade through the sheet with the heel of your hand, then cut.

There are many specialty saws which I could mention, but the above are likely to be the ones you will find most useful. My advice, use the proper saw for the job.

Levels: You may want to have two different levels in your toolbox. Remember, the longer the object to be leveled or plumbed, the longer the level should be to get an accurate reading.

The 12-inch or Torpedo Level: Some have a magnetic edge, to attach to metal surfaces. This makes them ideal for installing suspended ceilings, steel posts, and heating ducts. Some come with a battery-operated light for working in low-light areas.

The 24-inch level: This level is used for most other work. However, if you are doing a large deck or long fence you should use a 72-inch level.

Planes: This tool is used to smooth all surfaces of a piece of wood. To learn the proper use of a plane takes hours of practice. Most handypersons find that they are not skilled at using a wood-plane. If you plan to do a lot of hand woodworking, and want to do hand planning then a 6-inch plane, block plane, or tabletop plane is necessity.

Surform Plane: I find this tool to be the handiest for me because it is fool proof. Using a Surform plane does not take hours of practice. Many people refer to this type of plane, as the "cheese grater" plane because it looks like one.

Pipe cutter: This tool is invaluable for cutting pipes, plastic or copper. If you are going to do any plumbing, it is a must. It comes in several sizes and the small one works very well in tight places, such as between studs. Some plumbers and handypersons, use a fine-toothed miter saw to cut plastic pipes. I find this leaves a ragged edge, which is not acceptable to me.

Pliers: I recommend several types of pliers for your toolbox.

Side-cutting Pliers: are a good general tool. They work like pliers but also have a wire-cutting edge.

Adjustable pliers: Most commonly called channellock pliers they can be adjusted to many sizes of material. These pliers come in various lengths; find the length which suits your needs.

Locking pliers: When you need that extra hand, these are the ones to use. They lock around a nut or pipe, for a firm hold. These are commonly called, Vise-Grip pliers, which, by the way, is a brand name.

Needle-nose pliers: These types of pliers are pointed and are used for fine work. They come in many different shapes and sizes; they even come with a right-angled jaw. Select the type and size best suited for your needs.

Wire Stripping Tool: Although these are not strictly pliers, they fit nicely into this part of the list. Use this tool when you are doing electronic or electrical work. The jaws are graduated to fit the size wire of various gauges and will cut the insulation, but not the wire, when adjusted properly.

Retractable Knife: An indispensable tool for any toolbox. It can be used for cutting almost anything from thin plastic to wallboard to… well, even your fingers. I suggest the retractable-blade type, as they are safer to use. Be very careful when using this type of knife. I found out, by accident, that a sharp knife blade in my pocket is dangerous to my health.

Stud Sensor: This electronic tool is the only tool I have found which will accurately find studs, or floor and ceiling joists. The sensor measures the density of the surface. When the sensor is moved across the surface and comes to a denser area–joists or studs–it beeps and a red light comes on.

Hand or Electric Drills and Screwdrivers: You will have to drill a hole or put in or remove screws many times. An electric drill or electric screwdriver, with wood, steel and masonry drill bits, will be labour savers. Our forefathers used the push-pull, or the "eggbeater" type of drill. Most handy people have put these into the antique tool-box by now.

Wood and Masonry Chisels: Several sizes of masonry-chisels, sometimes called cold chisels, and wood-chisels will be a much-needed addition to your toolbox. Select the chisel best suited to your use. If you are going to pound a wood-chisel with a hammer or mallet then purchase a chisel with a reinforced handle.

Tool Pouch: A quality, leather, tool pouch will save pockets in your jeans, and save many steps to retrieve the tool you need. I have used the same pouch since 1960 when my wife and I built our first house.

There are many other tools which will come in handy, but which are not a necessity, unless you are going to do a job which requires that special tool.

I hope this list will help you outfit your toolbox

The best piece of advice my Grandpa Mac ever gave me about buying tools was, "Buy the best and you'll get what you deserve. Buy the cheapest and you deserve what you get."

Author's note: SharpTooth, Wonderbar, Surform are all trademarks of Stanley Tools International.

Chapter 11

Handy Tips
or
Stuff I Learned the Hard Way

Most of us begin our adult life knowing how to do things around the house but I had a head start on most people.

From the time I was knee-high to a grasshopper, and stood at my Grandpa Mac's workbench while he "did his thing", with tools, I was always learning. I learned how to straighten nails, sand wood, fill holes, and solve problems. As I grew and faced problems of my own I realized the value of Grandpa Mac's advice and instructions. One of the things I learned from him was how to look at a problem from outside the box, look for solutions, which were not obvious.

In this chapter I have shared some of the handy tips I learned from solving my own problems. I include solutions other people have shared with me. To these people, I say "thank you".

All of these solutions have worked for me. I must caution you, however, that you may find some solutions to be unworkable. I suggest you look at your particular problem from outside the box and use these tips **as a guide only**. Each problem is unique and only you can really solve the puzzle.

I would like to say a word about the illustrations in this chapter. Several years ago, when I was writing for newspapers and magazines, I wanted to provide capsule solutions to some common problems. Using a photo to illustrate the problem and the solution was not practical. Many of the details were lost or pictures were almost impossible to take because of the locations. My late friend, George

Balbar, suggested I take the best pictures I could from which he said he would then make an artist's interpretations.

However, I was not good with a camera, and lighting the areas was difficult. Along came Wayne Farrar, another friend, who was a professional photographer. He was not always available to take the photos, so he taught me to take better photos. I used black and white film and a simple camera with a flash. The results of the efforts of these two friends can be seen throughout the book. I am just sorry that George and Wayne are not with us today and able to see the results. I doff my hat to my two dear, late friends and say, "thank you".

Handy Tip #1–Cleaning Stains from Plastic Laminate Counters

"Did you see the stain on the counter top here in the kitchen?" I hear my wife call.

Stains on a plastic laminated counter top can be removed by applying rubbing alcohol. Let stand for 10 minutes, wipe clean with a dry cloth.

"Yeah. It must be from the plastic milk bag. I'll clean it off right away."

"It's okay. I'll do it; I'm here in the kitchen."

If you spill wine, tomato sauce or grape juice on the counter, leaving a stain, it will not be a pretty sight. Stains happen more often on older laminate tops because the clear–protective coating has worn off and the stain bonds to the unprotected under layer.

"Dear, it won't wash of with soap and water. What can I use, cleanser?"

"No, don't use any thing which might scratch; you could mark the surface even worse. I have the solution to the problem right here."

Rubbing alcohol usually does the trick. Pour a little on the surface and let it stand 15-20 minutes. In most cases you will find the stain lifting as you pour the alcohol on the surface. Wipe it off with a damp cloth. The stain should be gone. If it is still there–but much diminished–repeat the process. The stain should go after one or two applications. If it does not disappear, then it is time to install a new top.

The tools and materials required are: a sponge or cloth and rubbing alcohol.

Handy Tip #2–Caulking a Bathtub

Replacing the caulking around the bathtub is something which we all must do at one time or another. If done correctly it will not be as often.

"I pulled my job for this weekend from the Job Jar, dear. Looks as if I am going to be caulking the bathtub."

"Please don't make the mess you did the last time. It took you three days to clean up," she responded.

Have you ever been caught up in this very messy job? Needless to say I have, many times. In the early years I used a popsicle stick for smoothing off the caulking and ended up with caulking from stem to stern. There was caulking here, and caulking there, and bits of caulking everywhere.

"I'm going over to your brother's place first," I called out.

"What are you going there for?"

"I told him when I was going to caulk our bathtub, I would go over and do his first," was my answer.

You see, it takes practice, this caulking job, so I had offered to do my brother-in-law's tub first. That way I got to practice and the mess was at his house. Hey, he is getting it done for free, so he should not complain!

When you have perfected the method, do your own tub. This applies to caulking old windows as well.

As my father once said, "There are two ways to do a thing: the wrong way and my way". Now I am not saying my way is the only way, but I have found it works for me and it should work for you. You will not have to get someone to peel your clothes off of you after you are finished, either.

If you read the instructions on the tube of caulking you will likely find the manufacturer says, "Cut off the end of the spout on an angle, and then, as you squeeze the caulking out of the tube, draw it along the crack in which you are putting the caulking."

The problem with this is the caulking will just lie there in a convex bead, on the surface and will not be forced into the crack. If the caulking is not forced into the crack it will not stay in place, and you will be doing it all over again in another year. I have found, by cutting the caulking spout straight across and then **pushing** the tube along the crack you will force the caulking into the crack ahead of you. At the same time the caulking will be smoothed into a convex, or cove shape. This means once you have mastered the procedure there will be no need to smooth off the bead of caulking–hence no mess.

By the way, the best tool for smoothing caulking is your finger. If you find a need to smooth the caulking be sure to have some **clear**, liquid dishwashing detergent handy, in a small dish, for lubrication. Dip your finger into the liquid, then smooth off the caulking. The detergent will keep the caulking from sticking to the finger, it will also act as a lubricant. When you have smoothed the caulking wipe the excess on a cloth, (paper towel can be used but I find it is not as satisfactory as an old cloth) which you can throw away later.

I said use **clear** liquid dishwashing detergent.

"Dad, it's Jim," my son is calling for some advice.

"Yes, my boy, what is it–and if it's money I don't have any," I quip.

"I caulked the new shower enclosure, I heard you say to use liquid dishwashing detergent for a lubricant. Does that work?" Jim asks hesitantly.

"Yes, it does why do you ask?"

"Why did my caulking turn green?"

"Why did you use a green dishwashing detergent?" I asked

"How did you know that was what I used?" he asked me, almost stunned by my revelation.

"The stain is green, thus the detergent had to be green," was my simple comeback.

Evidently he had not listened to me completely, as children have been known to do sometimes.

He had a green stain on the white caulking, and it could not be washed off. This meant he had to remove all the caulking and start again. So, stick to clear, liquid detergent.

Note: When removing caulking you must scrape all of the old caulking from the crack, and then make sure the area to be caulked is clean and dry.

The tools and materials required are: old screwdriver, tile and tub caulking, vinegar, clear or white liquid dishwashing detergent and clean cloths.

Handy Tip #3–Help with Paint and Varnish Removing

If you have ever refinished a piece of furniture, you will know the mess the soft paint or varnish makes. When stripping a piece of furniture everyone faces the problem of getting rid of the old, softened paint or varnish, after scraping. Here is an interesting solution to that problem, and probably one of the best tips I have ever been given, regarding this dilemma of getting rid of the old, soft and messy paint or varnish.

I learned this tip from an antique dealer in Niagara Falls, Ontario. He was stripping an antique chest one day when I went into his shop to talk to him about a piece of furniture, I was restoring.

I watched as he scraped a big wad of paint from the chest. Where was he going to put the old paint? He picked up an old juice can and scraped it into the can, then went back for more. I did not know how he did it. I could never get rid of old paint into a juice can; round can, flat blade–they do not match.

When refinishing, it is easier to scrape the knife off on a stiff wire as shown, not on edge of can!

"I wish there was a better way to get rid of the old paint. I have scraped it into a can, like that, but because the edge of the can is round and the scraper is flat it just doesn't seem to work. I end up with most of the scrapings falling off onto the floor. I have tried old newspapers and cloths but that is even messier. If only there were square cans to give me a long straight edge on which to scrape the blade of the scraper," I said to him.

With a wry smile he said, "I never have any trouble getting the old paint into the juice can".

I looked into the can and noticed all the old, messy, soft paint had fallen into the can and none down the outside. How could that be I wondered.

So, being the inquisitive one that I am, I asked, "How did you do that?"

"I use a short piece of wire coat hanger, just about two inches longer than the width of the can. Then I punch holes in the can, close to the top on either side, and run the wire through, bending each end over on the outside. Now, I have a straight edge on which I clean my scraper," he explained.

When he is done he puts the full can of waste in with his hazard-ous–waste material for disposal. A great idea, and one which I have used hundreds of times. Try it; I know you will like it.

The illustration above shows how he did it.

The Tools and materials required are: old juice can, piece of wire coat hanger.

Handy Tip #4–Sanding Wood–the Finer Points

After you have stripped the paint or varnish from a piece of an-tique or collectible furniture you may be tempted to sand it. My advice is simple–**Do not sand it.**

Sanding an antique, or collectible, will lower the appraised value. I know this from experience. Sanding will remove the "aged" look of the piece–the patina–and the value of it will go down, way down.

Our first piece of antique furniture was a jam cupboard, which my mother and father bought for my wife for her birthday. When my father saw it, he asked me why she wanted that piece of "junk".

She really had an eye for antiques and collectibles, and she saw the potential in the jam cupboard.

It took me about three years to get around to stripping it. Frankly, I was afraid of the job. I had never stripped paint or refinished fur-niture. The piece had about seven coats of paint on it. The first coat, the one next to the wood, was a lead-based paint. (It has been dem-onstrated that lead-based paint can be dangerous to your health and the experts suggest wearing a respirator while working with this type of paint.) Once all the old paint had been removed, down to the bare wood, we could see where, in years past someone had set jam or pickle jars on the bare wood; there were black jar rings, which were quite visible. My wife thought they were ugly and detracted from the piece.

The colour of the wood was a mellow, aged pine, with the rings, "foot prints from the past", or "history". We know that now, from our experience with antiques, but then we did not.

"I don't like the colour of the wood or the jar rings, I would like it sanded," my wife said.

Remember, at this time, we had no knowledge of antiques, their value or how to refinish them. I performed four "no-nos" on this cupboard and we lost over $300 in value because of them.

Mistake number one. I got out the belt sander, and sanded the whole chest. Now it looked like new pine.

"I don't like the look of that white pine… it is too new looking," exclaimed my wife.

I agreed with her.

"What do you want me to do?" I asked

"Stain it," she suggested.

Mistake number two. I stained it.

Mistake number three. I changed the hinges, to new wrought iron hinges. I shudder remembering this because the old hinges had been hand-forged with handmade screws.

Mistake number four. I took the handmade, one-piece, wooden knobs off the drawers and doors. I replaced them with white porcelain knobs.

After that we began to collect antiques, became friends with a couple who were the antique dealers I mentioned earlier, and we learned a whole lot about antiques.

So, I repeat **no sanding** or **staining** antiques or collectibles.

However, if you have a piece of new unfinished furniture, or you have made a piece in the shop that you must put a finish on, you must sand it first.

With new wood, you will find that if it has been in the lumberyard or your shop for a while, it has, what I call, oxidized. The surface has dried, and turned a darker colour. I have been told you must "waken the wood up" by sanding. If you want to use a power sander, use an orbital one. A belt sander can really do some damage, if you do not know how to use it properly. Hand sanding for the final touch is best. When hand sanding use medium grit paper for the first sanding and extra fine for the final sanding. Do **not** over-sand, and do

not sand fast and hard: oils could come to the surface and may seal it unevenly. If this happens it will be difficult to get a stain to take uniformly. In fact, if it is hardwood, you may not even be able to get a stain to take at all.

Handy Tip #5–Applying a Finish

Never apply a finish in the room in which you have done the sanding… this is a "Hammar law". Dust will float, in the air, until you apply your first coat of finish… then whap, it hits the wet finish and you have to start all over again. A wet finish is like a magnet to dust in the air. Dust, created by sanding is your biggest finishing nightmare. The only way to remove the dust, from the surface of the furniture, is with a tack cloth. (To see what a tack cloth is and how it works read Chapter 6, page 60 Dust from Sanding.) Never vacuum or dust with a dry cloth. It only puts the sanding dust on the piece of furniture into the air. Wipe the tack cloth over the surface, and pick up the dust.

Next, if it is soft wood, apply a conditioner to all surfaces including the end grain. If it is hardwood, apply the conditioner to **all end grains only.** A conditioner partially seals the surface afterward allowing you to apply stain smoothly, and wipe it off to the depth of colour you wish.

Stain, in most cases, is not a final finish, it is simply a colour to give the wood some depth, and to enhance the grain.

There are many ways in which to apply a stain. Each manufacturer will give you staining instructions on their container. These instructions take precedent over any instructions outlined here.

I prefer to use a gel stain on my projects. It is easy to wipe on the surface and spread evenly. When applying a gel stain I always keep a separate cloth with which to wipe surplus stain from the surface giving me the desired depth of colour. With a liquid stain I prefer to use a cloth even thought the instructions may indicate using a brush. Wiping a liquid stain on my project, I find, gives me more control over the depth of colour achieved. A second cloth is always handy for wiping off the surplus stain on the surface.

Remember when choosing a stain that you can only make a piece of wood darker. That is a piece of dark walnut cannot be made white like birch by applying a birch stain. Birch, on the other hand, can be made to look dark like walnut by applying a walnut stain. There are as many types of stains as I have hairs on my head so I can only deal with the process of staining in a general way.

After staining is finished and has been allowed the proper drying time it is time to put a clear coat finish on the surface for protection. Sanding the stained surface can be done, but must be done lightly. If you sand with a heavy hand you will take some of the colour off the surface and it might look uneven in colour. Avoid sanding if possible.

Today, most clear coat finishes are made of polyurethane and give an excellent finish. I like to use a wipe-on poly, as it gives me that hand rubbed look. Because it is rubbed, or wiped on the surface, it goes on thinner and seems to dry faster.

Once the first coat of clear finish has dried, in a dust-free environment, it is time to sand in preparation for the second coat of clear finish. Between coats you must use extra fine steel wool or sandpaper, to smooth out the finish.

If you use Water-based poly do not use steel wool for smoothing. I have found that remnants of the steel wool left on the surface, will rust with the water-based finish. After sanding the finish use the tack cloth, then apply the next coat of finish, and so on, until the job is completed. For the number of coats of clear finish you require check manufacture's instructions, but three coats should be sufficient for most projects.

All the work you have done–to build the furniture, or to strip the furniture–will be wasted, if your finish work is not completed properly. Take your time. Keep the dust off the wet and tacky finish. Good luck.

The tools and materials required are: a tack cloth, brushes of a size suitable for the project, conditioner, a stain and clear coat finish of your choice, solvent to clean brushes and plenty of cloths for clean up.

Handy Tip #6–A Handy Stand for your Blow-Torch

I developed this handy little stand by chance. We moved into a new house in the late 60s, a split-level design. On the lower split there was a roughed-in bathroom. The plumber left about 10-inches of 4-inch copper drainpipe sticking up, where the toilet was to sit, upon which he had soldered a flattened piece of 4-inch copper drainpipe to seal it. When we decided to finish the bathroom I had to cut off

Make a handy stand for your torch from a piece of 4" drain pipe.

the piece protruding from the concrete floor. When I cut it I naturally set it down with the flattened end on the floor. It stood there until I started soldering the waterlines in place when I set the blowtorch into the old drainpipe–Shazam! Like magic an idea was born. You never can tell what little thing will come from just such a happening, so keep your eyes open. Who knows, you might just find something worthwhile for your shop.

I have made several drainpipe-stands over the years for friends to use. You can do something similar with black plastic pipe but you can not flatten a piece for the base. Instead, use a toilet flange for the base. The base is wide and it will make the whole thing more stable, as a blowtorch stand.

The tools and materials required are: a 9-inch piece of 4-inch copper drain pipe, a 6-inch piece of 4-inch copper drain pipe, blow torch and solder **or** a 9-inch piece of 4-inch plastic drain pipe and a plastic toilet floor flange.

Handy Tip #7–The Dripping Faucet

Drip… Drip… Drip… Drip! Loss of sleep, loss of concentration and loss of water, not to mention the cost of heating it and putting it down the drain.

If you have a dripping faucet it could be costing you all of the above. It is time to repair the faucet. Once, after I had talked about

fixing a faucet on my radio show, I had a listener ask what the big deal was about a dripping faucet. I told him I would do an experiment in the coming week and let him know what the big deal was on the next show.

I put a measuring cup under a faucet and set it dripping. I measured the amount of water collected in a ten-minute period, which was

5.3 ounces. This was almost enough water to fill my bathtub, once a week for a year.

If you have a dripping faucet there are several things affected by the drip: the porcelain, which will stain in time, your pocket book, not to mention a natural resource as well. If it is hot water dripping, not only have you paid for it through the water meter, but–paid the cost of heating it. And, if you pay for your sewers based on the amount of water you have used, you have paid for it again. What a waste, all for a fifty-cent washer. Fix it now!

The tools and materials required are: adjustable wrench, flat blade and Phillips screwdrivers, the appropriate size and configuration of washers for your faucet.

Handy Tip #8–Replacing a Faucet Washer

The preceding tip told you why to replace a faucet washer. This tip will tell you how.

Many of us still have faucets with washers in them. Washers should be replaced on a regular basis. I do not mean every six weeks or every year, but do not let them go until the faucet starts to drip. It could damage the seat and the sink.

Changing a washer is a simples operation. **First**, and this is important, **turn off the water feed to the faucet**. If you do not you could have a flood. At the very least you will take a shower at the faucet. The water shut-off, hopefully, is under the sink. If it is not, then you must turn the water off at the main, where the water line comes into the house. This can be a tough job if the main valve has not been turned off for some time. Be careful that you do not unthread the valve from the pipe. I do not say this to frighten you, but it is a remote possibility.

Once you have shut the water off, remove the handle from the faucet, by undoing the small bolt in the top of the handle. Sometimes you cannot see this bolt, because it is covered by a small cap with the letter "C" or "H" or with a cap coloured red or blue, denoting hot or cold. A small knife inserted under the cap pops it off.

Now, using a wrench, an adjustable crescent would be good, undo the nut holding the cartridge in the faucet. This is the large nut under the handle you have just removed. The cartridge will now slip out of the faucet body. Under the cartridge you will see a very thin washer sitting on the top of the faucet. This must be replaced when you put the faucet back together.

On the end of the cartridge there is a rubber washer. Undo the bolt holding it, as shown in the illustration above, and buy another washer just like it. I must point out here, there are flat top washers, and shouldered washers you must buy the proper one and the proper size. After replacing the washer it is a good idea, while you have the faucet apart, to replace the "O" ring. This is a rubber washer, which fits around the cartridge, just up from the bottom. It prevents the water from seeping out around the handle. While you have the faucet apart it would not hurt to check the "seat", for roughness and cracks. The seat is in the bottom of the faucet body. Just put your little finger into the hole in the faucet and feel the seat. It should be smooth and free from cracks. If it needs replacing then do it now. The seat, if rough, can damage the new washer very quickly. There is a special wrench for removing the seat; it is not expensive and is worth the investment. After all is complete it is time to put the faucet back together and turn on the water.

The tools and materials required are: adjustable wrench, flat blade and Phillips screwdrivers, the appropriate size and configuration of washers for your faucet.

Handy Tip #9–Saving the Chuck Key of an Electric Drill.

If the rubber holding the chuck key to your electric drill cord breaks you could lose it. How do you safeguard the key and keep it close at hand? I use a wide rubber band and loop it around the cord and key at the plug end of the cord.

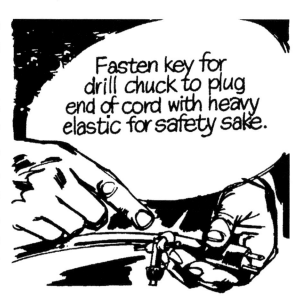

Fasten key for drill chuck to plug end of cord with heavy elastic for safety sake.

The original piece of rubber kept the key down near the plug. You may decide you want the key to be kept close to the drill, so it is handy. This is not a good idea–it is unsafe. The key must be kept near the plug, this reminds you to unplug the drill before you change a drill bit. Leaving the drill plugged in when changing a drill bit is extremely dangerous. Just imagine what would happen if, with the key in place in the chuck, you accidentally pulled the trigger. You could lose an eye, a finger or do other damage to yourself. **Always unplug the drill before inserting the key into the chuck!**

Handy Tip #10–Lubricating a Screw for Easier Driving

It is always difficult to put a screw into hardwood or, for that matter, into almost any wood. Drilling a pilot hole first certainly helps, but a lubricant makes driving smoother and easier. You cannot use oil as a lubricant because it will penetrate the wood and ruin

it. Grandpa Mac told me how he did it; and I know many other people use this method as well. Grandpa Mac used a slightly dampened bar of soap, rubbed the thread-end of the screw over the bar and then drove the screw home. You must wipe off the surplus soap as it oozes from the hole. This allows you to put a finish on the wood, as the soap will

Before putting screws into hardwood, rub the screw on soap bar first. This adds lubrication to the threads...making job easier!

not prevent the penetration of finish. It works for me and I know it will work for you. I keep small, used, bars of soap in my toolboxes.

It has also been suggested that candle wax can be used but I have found this not as mess-free as the soap. Also, wax can not be wiped away with a damp cloth. If you want to use the candle method here is how it works: light a candle, let it burn for a couple of minutes–a small pool of liquid wax accumulates at the base of the wick. Dip the screw in this wax and then drive it home into the wood. I think you can see how messy and inconvenient this method can be.

Handy Tip #11–Matching Wall Switch Plates to your Wallpaper

This is about adding a special touch to your decorating job. After spending many hours hanging wallpaper, you then put the switch and receptacle plates back on the wall. The ivory, white or brown,

plates may not add anything to the overall look. In fact, they can take away from the beauty of the job you have just completed. I have found my eye, drawn to plates because the colour is so different to that of the wall covering.

In a decorating store, my wife found clear plastic plates with steel or aluminum inserts. The inserts can be painted to match the paper, or covered with some of the paper. Applying the paper to the insert is not quite as easy as it sounds, but definitely worth the time. Cover the metal plate, insert it into the clear plastic cover, then install the whole package onto the electrical box, just as you would any other plate. Be sure to line up the wallpaper pattern in the plate with the paper on the wall around the electrical box.

Another interesting touch is to cover the plate with some of the material from the drapes or throws in the room. If the material is very different from the wallpaper, it may stand out like solid coloured plates, but at least it matches something in the room. This extra attention to detail with the wall switch-plates sets your decorating job apart from the ordinary.

The tools and materials required are: a screwdriver suited for the bolt used in your switch or duplex plate, clear plastic switch or duplex plate kit.

Handy Tip #12–Insulate Your Basement = Energy Savings and Comfort

It has been said, most of the heat in a basement or crawl space escapes over the top of the concrete or block wall. I believe this to be true, generally. Of course, if there are windows in the basement, you must deal with them as an area of heat loss as well, but, back to the top of the basement wall. I am assuming the top of the wall was not insulated during construc-

tion. If you look closely at the top of the wall, you will see there is a mud sill on which the floor joists sit. The subfloor is nailed on the top of the joists. Depending upon when the house was built there was either mortar or caulking put under the mud sill as a draft-stop. It was put there to keep the heat from escaping under the sill, and to keep cold air from coming into the basement under the sill.

Insulate the top of basement walls... keeps basement warmer, saves on heating!

If your home was built when mortar was being used for a draft-stop then you should caulk here. The mortar breaks down with the expansion and contraction of the foundation and the wooden members of the framing.

Caulk along the top of the basement wall, where the mud sill sits. Then, caulk **between** the subfloor and the ribbon joist, and around the **ends** of the floor joists where they meet the ribbon joist. The caulking will stop the flow of air in either direction. Next, cut pieces of R28 insulation, fit them between the joists and the subfloor, and down over the mud sill. Simply putting insulation in this cavity, without caulking the cracks, will **not** do the trick completely.

Batt insulation, generally, is not an air barrier, it is a thermal barrier. A thermal barrier is one which impedes the flow of heat or cold not the flow of air. An air barrier stops the flow of air through cracks and holes preventing drafts. This is why you **must** caulk around the mud sill and the ends of the joists.

Now, cut pieces of poly vapour-barrier, to cover the insulation, and staple it to the subfloor at the top, and the joists at the sides. As well, seal the top, bottom and sides of the vapour barrier to the construction members, with a bead of caulking or acoustic cement along the edges and seams. Your wall-top is now insulated; you will feel a difference in the basement temperature each winter and welcome the difference in the warmth of your floors and basement.

Today's houses, under most building codes, **must** have the top of the basement wall insulated and sealed at the time of construction. This is the easiest time to have it done because there are no wires or plumbing pipes in the way. If you wish to save more energy, insulate basement walls as well. Check with your local building inspector to see what the code is in your area, for this job.

The tools and materials required are: R28 insulation batts, 6ml poly vapour barrier, staples and staple gun, caulking or acoustic cement, measuring tape and knife to cut vapour barrier and batts.

Handy Tip #13–Painting Preparation: do it Right the First Time

The foundation of a good paint job is important. If preparation is poorly done, the paint job will not last. Many people just brush off loose paint, and start painting. This is okay if you want to do it again next year. All good painters will agree, scraping all the loose paint off the surface, and then sanding the edges smooth around the old paint, is a must. If you do not sand the edges they will show up, as sharp lines when you apply new paint. Most times, after scraping, you will be down to bare wood.

The reason the paint blistered and peeled was likely moisture in the wood. The moisture could have penetrated into the wood from the outside, but most often it is from humidity in the interior of the home. On the outside, the sun will draw the moisture to the surface, cracking and blistering the paint, thereby allowing the moisture to escape.

If, after sanding and scraping, you are down to the bare wood it is absolutely necessary to prime, before the finish coats are applied. Primer seals and protects the wood, giving the new paint a surface to which it can bond. After priming apply your finish coat. Most primers come in white, however, I suggest you buy a primer which can be tinted. Have the primer tinted a couple of shades lighter than the finish coat. This allows you to see where you have applied the finish coat and you can then be sure you have covered all of it. If the primer is white it will make the finish coat look lighter than the colour you selected.

Always use good quality paint and brushes. Clean the brushes before storing them. (See Chapter 3, page 25, Speed Cleaning Paint Brushes.) You will not regret it down the road.

The tools and materials required are: stiff paint scraper, good quality paintbrush, brush cleaner, primer paint.

Handy Tip #14–Filling a Crack in Concrete

So, you have a crack in your concrete foundation–what to do? I guess the obvious answer is "fill the darn thing"–easier said than done.

In my early days in the lumber business I asked a contractor how to fill cracks in concrete. Remember, this was in 1951; the products we use today were not available to us then. He told me to use a cold chisel for this job and make the crack into a "V" shape. This I did, but he should have told me to make it an **inverted** "V", and then fill the crack, with a concrete mixture. Things have changed since then.

Brush water on a crack before patching, you will get better adhesion!

People still do the chisel trick, widen the crack into a "V" shape, then fill it with a sand, cement and water mix. Later they ask me why it did not stay in place. The answer is they used the wrong material and wrong method, as I did years ago. Sand, cement and water alone will not bond to the sides of the crack.

Crack filler, made especially for cracks in concrete, is the product to use. This crack filler must have hydraulic cement as one of its ingredients. Hydraulic cement expands as it sets, putting pressure on the sides of the crack, holding itself in place. Here are the steps I follow now when repairing a crack in concrete.

First, I use a concrete chisel, or old screwdriver kept for this purpose, to clean out the loose concrete. It is not necessary to make the crack a "V" shape groove, to accommodate the filler. In fact, it is detrimental to do so. Since the hydraulic cement expands sideways it needs straight walls to press against. If you chisel a "V" shaped crack the hydraulic cement will lift itself out of the crack.

Second, when you have scraped the loose concrete out of the crack use a vacuum cleaner with a crevice tool, and vacuum the dust out of the crack. With a clean paintbrush, apply clean water to the crack, just before pushing the crack filler into place. The water will soak into the dry concrete, keeping it from sucking the water out of the crack filler; it will also, pull the filler into the porous concrete by osmosis. Smooth off the filler and you are finished.

Most crack fillers are fast-set fillers and the instructions will likely say, "Mix with cold water". I found, by experimenting, the reason for using cold water. I used hot water one time, and the material set hard before I ever had it completely mixed. Read the instructions before you start the job. All manufacturers write instructions for the use of their products, and they supersede any instructions I have given here.

The crack filler is always going to be a different colour from the concrete, so you will have to live with the difference. You can try a concrete colourant in the mix to bring the patch material close to the original colour. A tricky job, but it can be done.

The tools and materials required are: cold chisel or old screwdriver, vacuum cleaner with crevice tool, stiff 2-inch putty knife, small tin of cold water, clean paintbrush, concrete crack filler which contains a hydraulic cement.

Handy Tip #15–Cleaning and Polishing Ceramic Tile

Ceramic tile looks great on a shower wall: it shines and sparkles giving you a feeling of a very sanitary place. But it will not last. After many showers the walls look dull, not as sparkly and bright as they once did.

There are several things you can do to keep the walls looking new. There are products on the market you spray on the wall before the shower and wipe off after the shower, to keep it looking new. Just wiping down the tile after a shower will keep it looking good as well. I use a window squeegee to take the surface water and soap off the wall; it works like a charm.

To polish ceramic tile use a silicone spray according to instructions on the can. It also seals grout lines.

Use a sealant spray to clean and polish your tile, about once a month or so depending upon how many showers are taken. It seals the grout, so it does not absorb the soapy water, and it polishes the tile. It also leaves a thin coating to protect the tile from dull soapy build-up. Regular maintenance of your ceramic tile will keep it looking new for years and years.

Handy Tip #16–The Proper Use of a Wood Chisel

What do you reach for when you are going to paint and have to open the can? What then do you use to stir the paint with before painting? Why the screwdriver, of course! Not the right tool for either job. Now, what do you reach for when you have a slotted screw to tighten or loosen? The screwdriver, of course. But it is covered with paint, so you reach for the chisel which is right there in front of you. Easy, right? It may be easy but it is the wrong tool for the job.

The wood chisel and screwdriver are probably the most misused tools in our toolboxes. The poor screwdriver is used for everything from a paint stirrer to a pry bar, and, oh yes, occasionally for putting in and taking out screws. The wood chisel is also used for everything from a screwdriver to a paint scraper. A wood chisel is for chiseling wood and nothing else. Now, there is a novel idea! Properly used it takes off corners, gouges out wood, smoothes off pieces of wood and helps make joints fit well, among other things.

Sometimes a handyperson, not you of course, but someone else, uses a hammer to drive the wood chisel. If you have to strike the wood chisel with a hammer, to take out the piece of wood, you probably are trying to take out too much wood at one time. However, there are projects when you must cut into the surface of a piece or make a square hole in which to fit another piece of wood. A rubber or wooden mallet can be used to strike the wood chisel gently. I prefer the heel of my hand, as shown below. If you use the heel of your hand you will not strike the wood chisel too hard–it will hurt.

There are wood chisels on the market with reinforced handles. You can strike these with a hammer, but you must be sure you have this kind.

Always pound a chisel with the heel of your hand or rubber mallet...saves the chisel handle!

My Grandpa Mac gave me some of his chisels for my workshop. One day when he visited my workshop he saw one of the wooden handles on "his" wood chisel all mushroomed out, in splinters. Boy, did I get a lesson on how to use a wood chisel and my responsibility to my tools.

I always remember his words. "Michael if you treat your tools right they will treat you right."

I have never forgotten this lesson. Grandpa Mac always tried to teach by example, I know I had seen him strike the wood chisel with his hand, but I was in a hurry and… well, what can I tell you–I goofed. I keep that chisel as a reminder of how stupid and thoughtless I was, with my tools, sometimes.

Handy Tip #17–Clean Furnace Filter Regularly or How I made a Fool of Myself

In 1977 "The Biggest" and worst snow storm in the recorded history of the region, hit Niagara Falls, Ontario, and the surrounding area, with a vengeance. There have been books written about that

storm. T-shirts saying I survived the storm of '77, have been printed and people still talk about it, around their fireplace every winter.

I lived in Niagara Falls and worked fifteen minutes down the highway, in the city of St. Catharines. The storm hit on a Friday afternoon; I was unable to leave St. Catharines because all the highways into Niagara

Falls were closed. There were drifts as high as a house. The wind blew and the temperature went down, down, down. The wind chill factor was out of sight.

I could not get home so I called a friend, Jean, and asked if my daughter, two of her friends, and I could stay with her. She was happy to have someone else in the house because her husband, Mat, who commuted the other way to Niagara Falls, could not get home. My wife opened our home to Mat and several other teachers.

Now that I have set the scene, let me tell you what happened. Jean's house began to get cold in the night; the furnace was just not putting out the heat. When I got up in the morning, the temperature was still falling outside and was nearly down to 50-degrees in the house. I called the gas company to ask if they could send someone out to look at the furnace, as there was a baby, only 6 weeks of age, in the house. They were swamped with calls but gave us priority.

When the service man arrived he went straight to the furnace air-filter and pulled it out. It was clogged with dust: only a hole the size of a Looney was letting air pass through (Jean and her husband had only moved in a few months before, they had not looked at the filter.) Once the filter was replaced the house heated up quickly. I tried to hide my red face–I was so embarrassed. Here I was, a home-improvement expert and radio celebrity, one who preached over and over, one should clean the filter–regularly, and I forgot to look there first.

The moral of this story is; **Clean the air filter in your furnace regularly!** Yes, even in the summer when the air conditioning is running. It is amazing how much dust does collect over a short period.

Handy Tip #18–Dangers of Dumping Water Beside the Foundation

The illustration shows water from the downspout pooling beside the foundation, which can cause big problems, in the basement.

Downspouts are meant to route the water from your eavestrough to the ground. Without them the water would fall directly from the trough to the ground and erode the soil, leaving a big hole in your yard. Useful as the downspout is, if it just "dumps" the water on the ground beside the foundation, the water will eventually find its way into the basement. If your soil is clay, the water could run down between the soil and the foundation until it finds a weak spot in the founda-tion, then, comes in. With sandy soil it filters down to the water table.

Even then, it could find its way into your basement. If your basement is finished with drywall or paneling you are in big trouble.

I did a calculation once, to see how much water would come off my roof in a year. In the area where I lived I found the water coming from my roof annually was enough to fill a twenty-four foot, round swimming pool, up to the two foot level. That is one heck of a lot of water.

The simplest way to get rid of the water is to lead it away from your foundation with a section of downspout. Connect a ten-foot section of downspout to the end of the downspout with an elbow such as the one in the illustration. The water will then flow out onto your law 10-feet further from your foundation. Using this system, however, you will have the job of taking off the downspouts, and putting them back on, whenever you cut the grass.

I have used two other systems and they are:

1) Put an underground drainpipe to a low spot in the back yard.

2) Dig a dry well in the yard.

#1 At my house I was fortunate to be able to put a drain pipe underground and direct the water to a low area in my back yard. I dug a trench two feet deep from my downspout to the low area in the yard. I connected a piece of perforated weeping tile, sometimes called "Big O", to the downspout and the water now runs to an area forty feet away from the house. Since my yard has very sandy soil the water seeps quickly into it and there is never a puddle.

#2 To make a dry well a 45-gallon drum is required, rocks about the size of a tennis ball and crushed stone–along with a strong back and a good shovel. Dig a hole larger than the barrel; it needs to be deep enough to allow you to cover it with about a foot of soil. Punch holes in the sides and bottom of the barrel, put a foot of crushed stone in the bottom of the hole, drop the barrel into the hole, and fill the barrel with the rocks. Pour the crushed stone around the barrel, put on the lid, put sod on top and you have a dry well. But, if your soil is clay then forget about this method: too much work and too hard on the back. Besides that, it will not work very well, if at all, because the water will not percolate out of the dry well.

Most basement water-problems stem from improper downspout-placement or dumping water right next to the foundation on an unsealed driveway or sidewalk. See the next tip for advice on sealing leaks at these problem spots. (See also Chapter 5, My D-I-Y Misadventures… item 5 "Speaking of Downspouts")

I have outlined just a few ways to divert the water from your foundation. There are several products on the market, such as the vinyl tube with a spring in it. This tube is rolled up to the elbow and when enough rain comes down the downspout the vinyl tube rolls out onto the law and dumps the water. When it stops raining the tube rolls up again.

The tools and materials required are: for system #1) 3/4-inch crushed stone enough for the project, water washed rock 2-inch to 4-inch in size, sufficient perforated-plastic weeping tile for project, long handle shovel, wheelbarrow, sod cutter or square mouth spade.

Handy Tip #19–Sealing your Driveway and Foundation

Despite having led the water from your eavestrough away from the house, does the water find its way into your basement? Is your basement a swimming pool in spring?

Where could it possibly be getting into the house now? There is an area which many people overlook, when it comes to keeping water out of the basement. It is the space between the driveway, or sidewalk, or patio and the foundation. If any of these areas happen to slope toward your house, and are directly adjacent to the foundation, you are asking for a leak in the basement.

When concrete or asphalt is laid next to a foundation the contractor should put an expansion joint between the new surface and the foundation wall. This expansion joint allows the two surfaces to expand and contract without affecting one another. This is why you may not have a leak for several years after a horizontal surface has been installed close to your foundation. But, what quite often happens is the expansion joint, over the years, deteriorates and disappears. This allows water flowing across the horizontal surface of the driveway, sidewalk or patio, to run down into the crack and find its way into the basement.

Simply putting some dirt or sand in this crack will not help. And you cannot successfully put concrete in the crack as it will not bond

You can help prevent water seepage by applying caulking between sidewalk and foundation.

easily and, when one of the surfaces expands, it will crack and you will have water flowing in again.

If the crack is no more than 1-nch wide and is deep I suggest you pour some fine, dry sand into the crack and fill it to within 2-inches of the top. Pack it down if you can. Now put a good flexible caulking in the crack. Be sure you purchase a caulking which is compatible, meant for the materials you have: concrete or asphalt. If the job is done correctly it should solve the water-leak problem for a long time.

There is also a rope like material, on the market which comes in a coil. It can be packed down into the crack. This material will not absorb water and acts as an expansion joint, sealing the crack. When I first saw a coil it reminded me of the rope caulking we used to use to seal the cracks in our old plank rowboat.

The tools and materials required are: old screwdriver, fine, dry sand, caulking of the type for your application.

Handy Tip #20-Dustless Sanding of Drywall Joints

Yes, you can actually "sand" drywall joints without creating dust. I guess I have rather misled you with the word "sand". I should have said "smooth" the joints of drywall, but that is not as dramatic a phrase.

In our first house, my wife and I installed over 2,000 square feet of drywall and we applied the joint system ourselves. This was in 1961 just before the advent of "premixed" or "ready mixed" joint compound. We had to mix it from the dry state with water and it is a messy job. My wife became proficient at the "art" of applying joint compound. I remember seeing her on a 2 X 6 plank, strung between two saw horses, as she did the ceilings: she danced along the 2 X 6 wielding a plastering trowel with the skill of a professional. Later we used a scaffold–much safer and easier. The mortgage company building inspector said, "She does a better job than the professionals".

After applying each coat of joint compound, (there are three in all) we had to sand the joint smooth. This, is very, very dusty. We wore dust masks. When we were finished, we looked like snowmen. In those days there were no tools designed to sand and vacuum up the dust of at the same time.

Use a wet sponge to smooth your drywall joints and cut down sanding dust.

There are three problems with using sandpaper.

1) The creation of dust, of course.

2) Over-sanding of the joint. Sometimes we over-sand and then the joint is too smooth. When the paint is applied, the joint becomes visible because it is smoother than the paper around it.

3) Sanding the paper surface, alongside the joint. If you roughen the paper alongside the joint, with the sandpaper, it is almost impossible to cover it up.

If there was a way to smooth the joint without any of these problems it would be wonderful would it not? Well, there is a way.

I was in contact with the sales representative for a gypsum company, as he called on our lumberyard on a weekly basis. We became good friends. During one of his visits I took him over to the house, to show him the job we had done with the drywall.

He was impressed and said, "I hope you used the wet sponge method instead of sanding the drywall."

"**What**?" was my response.

"A damp sponge, rubbed over the drywall joint, smoothes it out to the right texture: no roughing of the paper; no over-smoothing and best of all, no sanding dust."

He had forgotten to tell me about that method, before we started the "sanding"! Well, I know it now, and I pass it on for you to use.

If you talk to a pro drywaller he will tell you he likes the sanding method, but then he is not doing the sanding in his own house. He can leave the mess behind for you to clean up. By the way, when the furnace kicks in on the first cold day after you, or the pro, have sanded, there will be dust flying everywhere. So, clean out the ducts, before the cold weather.

The tools and materials required are: a thick utility sponge, bucket of clean water (change often).

Handy Tip #21–Spalled Concrete Repair

Many times we see a concrete sidewalk, steps, porch, driveway or garage floor, which has "spalled". (This is a flaking of the concrete surface.) It is generally, but not always, caused by salt, which has been brought to the driveway or garage floor by the car from the road. Sometimes the deterioration appears as small dusty flakes and sometimes it appears as larger thin shale-like pieces. Even though you sweep, hose down and work your hands to the bone, you will not get rid of the spalling. You must repair it.

With a special concrete patching material, containing a bonding agent, the repair will be quite easily done. Remember though,

the surfacing material you use will not be the same colour as the older concrete. Only resurfacing the whole area will provide a uniform colour, over the whole surface. If the proper patching material is used, you will be able to put a feather-thin layer on the old concrete.

The first time I used one of these special patching materials, I mixed the water in the quantity I would have used with ordinary sand-mix concrete. (Shamefully, I did not read the instructions first– just assumed I knew how to mix it.) I was putting it on a vertical surface, and with too much water in it, the patch sagged, and drooped; I had to scrape it off, while it was still wet, and start again.

The surface must be clean and free from dust, oil, dirt and salt. Use a wire brush on the surface to loosen any pieces which might flake off after or during the application of the surfacing material. Wash the surface with clean water using a garden hose and broom then let the surplus water evaporate.

The manufacturer of the surfacing material will likely give you very explicit instructions on the container for cleanup and preparation. **Their instructions take precedence over mine.**

Once the surface to be covered is clean, but damp, you are ready to mix the patching material for application. You cannot use ordinary sand-mix ready-mix concrete since the sand used is coarse and there is no bonding agent included in the mix, it will not be satisfactory. You need a bonding agent either included in the mix or to be added during the mixing. The sand must be a fine grind so the surfacing material will trowel out thinly. I have found if the surface to be covered is damp… **NOT** wet, no puddles or running water, the bond will be permanent. The material I used bonded well on a damp surface. **Always** follow the manufacturers instructions first.

I strongly urge you to read the instructions on the container and then follow them to the letter.

The tools and materials required are: garden hose, stiff scrubbing brush, concrete resurfacing material with a bonding agent,

(agent may be included in the dry mix or it may be necessary to add during mixing) and a concrete trowel.

Handy Tip #22–Removing Vinyl Floor Tile

Have you ever had to remove a vinyl tile floor? I have, and the method I am about to describe works well with most vinyl tile. However, in one of my removal jobs it did not work.

(See My DIY Adventures, Chapter 5, page 50… "We'll Just Spend a Few Bucks")

This is the first line of attack to remove old vinyl tile, as I see it anyway. I suggest you start in a doorway… it makes it easier to get to the edge of a tile and pull. Put a well-used dishtowel down on the

floor tile; use a thin one you do not want to use again. Apply a medium hot iron, as in the illustration, **do not use the iron directly on the tile**… this may ruin the iron. Yes! This is the iron with which your shirts are ironed. You may have to increase the temperature to make it work. It is easier to start with a low temperature and increase the heat than it is to set it too high and melt the tile. Iron the edge, four inches of the tile at a time, until the glue releases. With a stiff, wide putty knife under the tile start to lift and keep ironing. It works better if two people work at it. It is hard for one person to iron, push the blade under the tile and lift and pull all at the same time. It takes three hands to do it easily. Work on one tile at a time. If you get too anxious and start pulling on the tile before the adhesive releases you will break the tile off, this means starting over.

This same method works on many adhesives. It can be used in some cases to remove plastic laminate counter top material installed with some of the contact adhesives used a few years ago. If the tile or counter top does not release easily do not continue.

The tools and materials required are: clothes pressing iron, old, soft-cotton dishtowel, stiff 6-inch scraper or a square mouth spade.

Chapter 12

The Conclusion
or
Some Words of Wisdom, Finally

"It will add value to the house!" This is a popular misconception. What it really means is… we can spend a lot and get a little in return. Most of us believe, keeping up with the neighbours in decorating and renovating will add value to our homes. This is true if you do not overvalue your house. An overvalued house could be difficult to sell for its true price. On the other hand if the house you buy is smaller than the houses near it, or has been neglected and is run down you should upgrade it, bringing it in line with the neighbourhood values, makes it easier to sell. It will also make the neighbouring homes more valuable, so you have done the neighbours a favour.

My son, Jim, who is a handyman in his own right, has twice bought the "wart" in a neighbourhood and turned it into a beautiful home. Each became a home of which not only was he proud, but of which the neighbours were proud. He seeks out the worst looking house on the block, considers its potential, then goes to work on it. He upgrades the house with exterior and interior renovations. The value has now increased.

There is another popular misconception among many men. Since they are men, and men are "experts" in home improvements, they do not need to take advice from women.

Women reading this will think, "No, that's not the reason you feel that way. It's because you're a man and men can't accept helpful advice from women".

If there is only one piece of my advice in this book which you use let it be this one: Take advice from women and incorporate it into the way you do the project.

I can just hear you guys saying, "What are you crazy? If we take advice from a woman and we do it faster, and better, we will be bound to take their advice every time we start a project."

This may be true. But you know guys, if we **do** take their advice, we can blame them when it goes wrong. Hey, that sounds like a good plan! Do you think we can get away with it?

Throughout this book I have tried to give you an insight into my life, the life of a "guy" doing the stuff we guys have to try to do around the house. I have not always known how to tackle a project, but, with some creative thinking, I was able to solve the puzzle. If you look at the problems presented by your project, think out the possible solutions to those problems, you will complete it without too many errors.

Do not be afraid to ask for or take advice. Your wife, neighbours or friends can be of tremendous help. Talking the project over with them might help. Your local lumber or hardware store employs experienced people who are also more than willing to help you find a solution.

My son when he was only 15 years old went to work for a local retail lumber dealer, and discovered that people did not trust a "kid" to give them advice. Yes, he was only 15 years old when he started in the lumber business; but he already knew as much about building as many of the older staff members. What dumbfounded many a customer, was the fact that the older guy, the one they had asked for help–went to Jim for answers. When customers asked his age, he would answer, "I am 15 years old with 30 years experience". He had followed me around all his life and helped with the jobs around the house; he was well qualified to answer their questions. So, it may not always be the "gray-haired guy" in the store who knows the answers; it may be the young guy or girl.

Throughout the book I have made fun of the relationship between men and women on DIY jobs. I have known many women who were both the brains and the brawn on jobs. In my own case my former wife, worked hard on all of our projects and had many good ideas about "how to" when it came to building and decorating. Over the years, I have known men who have not had one iota of knowledge about the DIY jobs to be done. Your gender does not make you more or less qualified to do home repairs or renovation work. It is your desire and ability to learn that will make you the expert on the job.

Remember these words from Chapter 2, and make them your credo for any and all renovations and repairs.

Plan your work and work your plan.

Who Was Grandpa Mac?

Grandpa Mac was my maternal grandfather, a handyman extraordinaire. He was born, Norman Warren McGillivray, in April 1872. I felt Grandpa Mac was responsible for my interest in tools and wood–he taught me to respect tools and appreciate fine woods. Upon his death I inherited many woodworking tools, a collection owned by his father, my great Grandpa Mac, and Grandpa Mac. They occupied a place of honour in my home. I used many of them when my former wife and I built our first house in 1960. The collection is now in the possession of my son, Jim.

It was Grandpa Mac who taught me the art of problem solving, I often hear is words when I set out to solve a problem. He will always be here with me, guiding me and helping me with the many problems of home renovations and repairs. His love of fine woods rubbed off on me: as a result, I love to touch and work with exotic woods, whenever I can.

Grandpa Mac worked in railroading and served in the "Great War", 1914-1918. After returning from Europe he made his living for many years as a handyman. He made furniture and did home repairs for many of the residents of the city of Niagara Falls. With his skills, he was able to turn wood from packing crates and boxes into fine lamps, tables and chests. He collected hardwoods, air-dried them and used them in his furniture making.

My Grandpa Mac was truly, "one-of-a-kind".

Index

ISBN 141209449-6